Lisa —
It's fun working
with you!
Good luck with the
twins!

Jenny Montgomery

**I
CAN
PLAY**

I CAN PLAY

A Philosophy for Life

Gary Montgomery

Passages Publishing
Louisville, Kentucky

Passages Publishing
P. O. Box5093
Louisville, Kentucky 40205

First Edition

ISBN 1-886036-13-6

Library of Congress Control Number: 2001 132665

Book design and production
by Moonlight Graphic Works / Stephen Sebree

Cover photograph by David R. Lutman

CONTENTS

ACKNOWLEDGEMENTS

I owe many thanks to many people for enhancing my I CAN PLAY attitude as I worked on this book:

To the helpful members in the Kentucky Speakers Association, thank you for continuing to inspire me with your help, guidance and friendship.

To Ann Weeks, my publisher, thanks for pushing me to write my stories down.

To Ellen Schuhmann, my editor, thanks for doing a marvelous job making this speaker's stories come alive in the written word. Thanks also for listening to my stories.

To Tara and Troy, thanks for helping me grow by teaching me how to give. I received more joy from the two of you than I could ever have hoped for. I love you more every day. And thanks for letting me share our stories.

And to Judy, thanks for living my stories with me. There's never been a better coach, teacher, counselor or partner than you. I love you.

INTRODUCTION

For years I've known I was supposed to write this book, but I never knew why. I often wanted to write it, but continually asked myself what is it that I have to say that's meaningful enough for a book? Why do I need to put it into a book? What can I share with others?

Recently, while flying home after covering the University of Louisville Cardinals in a football bowl game in Boise, Idaho, I was reading M. Scott Peck's book "Further Along the Road Less Traveled." I realized that what I was reading is what he believes to be true--his stories and ideas in printed form. The book was more than entertaining, more than instructional. It was his philosophy, a collection of his beliefs, his life in print. Through his stories and ideas, M. Scott Peck came alive to me, and he believed in his philosophy so much he put it in writing for all to read.

This may not sound like a radical revelation, but it was for me!

I remember my English teacher from my first year of college. We were reading and discussing "The Oxbow Incident," a story of western lore in which an innocent man was hanged. The instructor suggested the story correlates to the crucifixion of Jesus Christ. I asked, "Can't people just write stories that entertain, stories that don't have underlying messages?"

"No," she replied, "because everyone has a message,

even if they don't know it. When you write, your message lives through the story."

I don't remember her name, I'm sorry to say. She was an excellent teacher because she taught me something I have never forgotten, even though I thought I had. Her message continues; it is alive in me.

When I share my stories, my message lives through them. It's a simple message: Success begins within by believing and trusting in yourself. Inside each one of us God has placed particular talents and abilities. Our path to success is shortened once we discover those talents and abilities and make use of them. I call that understanding, an attitude. I call it living life with an I CAN PLAY attitude.

Through my stories, you will receive my message. Some of the stories are entertaining, some are motivating, some inspirational, but most of all, they are me. Collectively they share the message I live.

I want the message to come alive in others; my children, my wife, my sister and brothers, everyone with whom I interact. I want them to see it, sense it, or feel it after being with me. And then I want them to try it because it works. Living life with an I CAN PLAY attitude gives us our best opportunity for success.

I guess I first discovered this attitude through sports. The most successful individuals were positive in their thoughts about themselves and their abilities. But this attitude transcends sports. It is alive in all aspects of life.

My hope is that the stories in this book lead you closer to discovering how great you can be. You already have the tools; they have been given to you. Your task is to use them to the best of your ability. The secret to success is discovering and using the tools, abilities and talents that are inside you!

As you read of the individuals and situations in my life, they may remind you of similar occurrences and people in your life. The situations I describe may give you a basis to compare with events in your own life, and, perhaps, to learn from and to grow. By reading and understanding my philosophy as it plays out in the stories, I hope it will assist you to form your philosophy of life. You will relive the stories in your own format, your own life message.

These are the stories that taught me that I could better believe in myself, that I can be the best I can be as I travel through life with an I CAN PLAY attitude.

I CAN PLAY

That's my favorite phrase, I CAN PLAY. And I'd like everyone to use it. Sometimes my audiences think I mean to have fun in life. That's a great idea, but it's much more than that. I CAN PLAY is all about creating a personal philosophy of life. The best way I can explain living life with an I CAN PLAY attitude is to tell the story of how it first came alive for me. My son, Troy, taught me.

THE RED SHOES

Troy has large feet. When he was younger we had to buy new baseball cleats each season because his feet kept growing. At the age of seven, we set out on our annual adventure to buy new cleats.

It's always fun to prepare for a new season, for it brings new adventures, new things to learn. I couldn't have guessed how much I was going to learn from this shopping trip.

We looked at black cleats, white cleats, white cleats with black trim, black cleats with white trim, but we were unable to find the ones Troy wanted. Finally, we saw them. They were on the wall shelf in the mall shoe store. Red baseball cleats.

Troy had never seen red baseball cleats, much less had them on his feet. He ran up to them with a wide-eyed look.

"Are those the ones you want?" I asked him.

"Yes, er no--I'm not sure, Dad," was Troy's reply. He really wanted the shoes. It was obvious. But he was worried about trying something new. Sound familiar?

My wife, Judy, and I watched our son walk around that store, looking at shoes, but continually coming back to the red shoes. We were sure those were the ones.

Finally, Troy made the decision. We sized his feet, got the ones that fit, admired the red shoes as he modeled them in the store, and headed home.

Once home Troy went straight to his bedroom. I wasn't up there, but I bet he put those shoes on his feet, bent down in his best shortstop stance, looked at the pretend batter in the corner of his room, and said, "Hit it to me. I can catch it," then glanced down to his new shoes and said, "Oh yeah, red cleats!" -- like the shoes were going to help him catch the ball!

And then he probably wrapped his hands around the bat he kept in his room, looked in the mirror, then at the pretend pitcher, and said, "I'm gonna rip this pitch!" And again looked down at the shoes and said, "Oh, yeah, red cleats!"

After about half an hour, Troy came downstairs. He had a troubled look on his face as he sat next to me on the couch, and asked the question that had been bothering him since he first saw the red shoes in the store. "Dad, do you think people will laugh at me when I wear these red baseball cleats on the field?"

At first I wished he hadn't asked the question. I remembered times people laughed at me, made fun of me when I tried something new, when I wanted to do something a little different, when I stepped up and stretched out after a goal no one thought I could achieve. I remembered all the times I was afraid to be myself, to step out and go after what I really wanted. I remembered the times I sat back and didn't go after the important things in my life, the times I thought someone might point at me and I would have to explain, and I didn't want to be put on the spot and explain myself or what I believed. It was always easier to just keep doing what I had always done in the past.

Why am I thinking all of this? It's just a pair of new shoes. Just tell him nobody will laugh. Just tell him to wear the shoes and if they do laugh, ignore them. Just tell him Mom and Dad think the shoes are nice. Or tell him we can take them back.

But I went in another direction. I told him the truth. "Troy, if you can't catch the ball or hit it or throw it, if you trip and fall when you run to first base, if you always stand back, waiting to be told what to do, if you aren't aggressive when you play the game, then people will look at you and say, 'There's Troy. And look at those silly red shoes he's wearing!' I could see Troy creating the picture in his mind.

"But if you can play the game. If you can hit the ball, if you always run as fast and hard as you can to first base, and the whole time you're thinking how you're going to get to second base ... and if you slide into second looking toward third, if you dive for the ball and never give up until the ball hits the ground, if you always show leadership to your team, and even to the other team, Troy, if you can play the game, and everybody sees you play the game, then everyone at the ballpark will point at you and say, 'Look, there's Troy! And look at those great red shoes he's wearing!'"

That's the truth. That's just the way it is!

Troy was listening intently. He was creating a vision, watching it unfold in front of him. After only a few seconds he jumped up and started out of the room.

"Hold on there, Bubba," I said. "What's the deal? What do you think?"

He turned, looked me in the eye, and very matter-of-factly said, "No problem, Dad, I CAN PLAY!"

What Troy did is what people do hundreds, no, thousands of times everyday. He determined what he thought of himself. He concluded that with his talent and his ability he would be able to deal with whatever would happen when he wore the red shoes on the baseball diamond.

I CAN PLAY! It was a little boy, no, a young man defining himself.

I wish I could have put what Troy was feeling into a bottle and sold it. Heck, I wish I could keep it with me all the time. But the truth is, it takes work to maintain an I CAN PLAY attitude.

I CAN PLAY! It was a defining moment, one I wish Troy to never forget. I knew immediately that I wanted my son to always remember how he felt about himself at that instant. We can't start too early in life believing in ourselves.

Understand this, Troy wasn't boasting. I've seen

boasting. I've seen kids, high school athletes, college athletes bragging how they were going to win, often without being able to back up the boast.

That wasn't what Troy was doing. He simply decided that after he examined who he was and what he was, he was comfortable wearing the red shoes. He was comfortable trying something new and prepared to deal with whatever came his way. After exploring his past and future on the baseball field, he decided he could play the game. And since he could play the game, he would wear the red shoes and just be himself. He said, "I CAN PLAY!" And once he decided he could play, the way he approached his problem was different. He was going to wear the red shoes with a positive attitude. That's the way to approach all issues. That's the way to travel through life, with an I CAN PLAY attitude.

My hope for Troy is that he always carries that I CAN PLAY attitude with him wherever he goes. I wish he could make it his personal philosophy—in high school, through difficult times in his college studies, when he embarks on a career, in personal relationships. It won't always ensure success, but it will always offer the best opportunity for success. I hope he will always be able to recall the feeling he had about himself that day when he matter-of-factly said, "I CAN PLAY."

When we approach life with an I CAN PLAY attitude, we're giving ourselves the best shot at success.

There are three key elements involved in developing an I CAN PLAY attitude:
- Creating Vision
- Building a Positive Atmosphere
- Taking Risks.

The stories and the ideas these themes lead to are grouped into sections. These are stories that can help further develop our vision, stories that will assist in building a positive atmosphere and stories that will encourage risk-taking.

When these are combined, they lead us to deeper self-belief and self-trust. That is the basis for success in all aspects of life.

CREATING VISION

People who live life with an I CAN PLAY attitude have vision. That implies seeing the outcome before it develops, or, more importantly, being able to decide circumstances in the present to determine outcomes in the future.

When I think of someone with vision, I see that person as wise, almost an all-knowing type individual. He or she appears to have a special sixth sense, as though the individual is capable of predicting outcomes in certain situations. Perhaps the word visionary would better describe how I think of this special quality.

People with vision know themselves so well that they can determine and decide the outcome of a situation, and how they will react, and help others react, even before it unfolds.

As they travel through life, they come to know themselves extremely well, and, since they know their strengths and their talents so well, they are self-confident. They are not self-serving, nor arrogant, but extremely confident and self-assured. So much so that they can step both into everyday situations and difficult situations with the same confidence. If, as they travel through everyday life, they encounter difficulties, they know and trust themselves well enough to adjust to obtain the best outcome possible. They made the best of any situation.

These individuals are not guided by outside influences, but are internally driven. They have explored and researched themselves and what they believe so that they know the truth about themselves and how they react to outside influences.

It's not that these individuals can predict or see the future. People with vision adapt to create the future. The future hasn't been created until they get there, and they understand that what they do today determines what will happen tomorrow.

Having vision starts with seeing ourselves as we are, knowing our talents, abilities, strengths and weaknesses.

QUESTIONS

Early each Saturday morning I gather with a group of men at McDonald's. It's sort of an accountability group. We discuss the past week, where we have been, and what we have learned. And we look forward to a new week, and what we can accomplish. It's accountability, responsibility, goal-setting and value adjustment. It's questioning ourselves.

It seems to me we need to continually question what we are doing, where we are headed, what we want to do, how we are going to get there, what skills we are going to use to arrive there, and how we will act once we achieve our goal. These all seem like worthwhile questions. And if we keep asking these questions, we keep our goal in sight.

So it seems a good idea to keep questioning!

I use four questions with audiences I speak to so they will continue to examine themselves and where they are headed. When I offer the questions to youngsters, they often look at me with that "what are you talking about?" stare. Here are the questions.

1. Who am I?
2. What do I believe?
3. What are my talents?
4. What am I doing with my talents?

I remember the first time I started asking these questions. They weren't in this format, but very similar.

When you stepped out the front door of the house where I grew up, and turned your head just slightly to the right, you were looking at Bucheit's Grocery. Mr. and Mrs. Bucheit had run the grocery for as long as I could remember--heck I was only about seven years old at the time, so I guess the grocery was always there for me.

I remember stepping in the front door of the old store and walking on the rough hardwood floors. The sound of my leather shoes on the old boards would echo against the walls. I remember Mrs. Bucheit's friendliness. She must have attended one of the first customer service seminars ever given because she knew how to make people feel comfortable! I enjoyed walking into that store, and I just assumed everyone grew up having a wonderful experience like Bucheit's Grocery across the street.

It never occurred to me that Bucheit's would ever close. But one summer afternoon I noticed Mr. Bucheit was moving equipment out of the store. The grocery didn't open for business the next day.

The building sat empty for about a month until some people showed up and started hammering and hauling in long benches. They painted the huge storefront windows white and in black letters they stenciled the words "GUIDING LIGHT MISSION."

I asked my mother what was going on, and she told me that Bucheit's Grocery would now be a church ... a storefront church.

I didn't understand how anyone could have services in a grocery. As a Catholic, the only churches I had been in were large, ornate, with huge altars and stained glass windows. It seemed peculiar to have church where I used to buy Popsicles and pickles.

As it turned out, their services were nothing like I had known before. Instead of the church organ that I was accustomed to, they brought in all sorts of music makers-- guitars, drums, tambourines. And sing! Wow! You could hear them on Wednesday night all the way down to Corbett's Gas Station at the end of the block. It's a wonder ol' Bucheit's Grocery was able to keep the roof attached!

I remember those Wednesday nights. Many times after our customary game of hide-and-seek, and a little peeking in at the Guiding Light Mission, after my friends David, Kenny and William had gone home, I would lie in the grass in my front yard. I still recall the softness of the green carpet and the peacefulness of watching the stars on the black canvas above me. All sorts of things raced through my mind—important things a seven-year-old would ponder. But my silent thoughts would be shattered by the sounds from across the street. It was time for the preacher to deliver his message in the storefront church.

I remember him asking the assembled folks, "Do you believe?" They answered, "I believe." He always asked the question twice. I assumed he didn't believe them or he had difficulty hearing.

"Do you believe?"

"I believe," they responded in unison.

Then there was a pause. I imagined the preacher leaning toward the people and looking them right in their eyes. Kind of like my Little League baseball coach would do when he wanted to make a point, or my dad did when he wanted to be sure I did what he told me.

Finally the silence would be broken when the preacher shouted, "What do you believe?"

And then another long pause. From there I must

have drifted off in thought. I asked myself, "What do I believe?"

As I stared into the night sky, I asked myself about my beliefs for the first time. It was the beginning of questioning myself, and pushing myself, and reaching for my goals. In a way it was the first time I asked, "Who am I? What do I believe? What are my talents? What am I doing with my talents?"

I'm sure you remember asking yourself those questions for the first time. It was probably a long time ago, in your youth, perhaps as a teenager. It may have been in church or at school. Perhaps your mother or father prompted the questioning, maybe a friend or a teacher.

It doesn't matter when it was. What does matter is that you continue asking. It's by asking questions and exploring the answers that the learning begins within.

 ## THE NEXT STEP:

Take some time alone and explore. Look at your talents, your gifts, your abilities and what you are doing with them.

Keep asking yourself the questions, Who am I? What do I believe? What are my talents? What am I doing with my talents? Some days you will like the answers, some days you won't. It doesn't matter. Keep asking. Keep answering.

Keep exploring yourself as well as your surroundings. It's by exploring that we grow and reach our potential. It's by exploring that we see who we are and create the vision to see where we are going.

And by the way, if you ever get the chance, join us at McDonald's on Saturday mornings. Come with plenty of questions. We've found that somebody will have all the answers.

REDBIRDS

The Redbirds were the best team in the league and probably the best team I ever coached. They had coasted through the league schedule and now faced the double-elimination tournament. The Redbirds had plenty of talent.

When these guys walked through the ballpark wearing their Redbirds' uniforms, young kids and parents alike would ask about their team. They became mini-celebrities, or at least they thought they were. Perhaps that's why they were beaten by the Royals in the tournament.

As we sat on the side of the hill following that loss, I saw some long faces. They knew they had the ability, but I think they knew that they hadn't given it everything they had. They thought they were the Redbirds, and they just needed to show up to win. Or perhaps they thought the coach should have had them better prepared.

I figured I had to do something to change their thinking. Adjust their attitudes. Get them back to being the Redbirds before another loss would bring a premature end to their season.

"Fellas, 25 years from now, you're going to look back at this baseball season and remember the Redbirds. When you do, what will you remember?" I really didn't want any answers. I only wanted to get their attention.

"Let's say you are over at a friend's house for a party. Everyone is gathered on the patio, telling stories from days gone by. Your children are on the swing set playing, and the hamburgers are on the grill. Someone is talking about his or her elementary basketball team and how talented the players were. Another friend tells about being part of a great band. And someone else relives his days as a member of a great football team.

"You let everyone else finish because when it's your turn you're going to tell them about the Redbirds. And when you tell them about the Redbirds, you know everyone will listen because of how special the team was and what it accomplished.

"You'll tell them about the games early in the season when the other teams couldn't even get a hit. You'll tell them about the hitting of this team, everybody on the team. You'll try to explain how everybody in Lyndon Park, from senior baseball to girls' T-ball talked about the Redbirds, and how the Redbirds played the game. Yeah, when this season is over, you'll tell people the Redbirds had plenty of talent. But you'll also tell them that the Redbirds worked hard, they played hard, and they enjoyed learning and playing the game.

"But then you'll get to the part where the Redbirds lost in the play-offs. You'll probably say that they lost because they didn't play up to their potential." I paused to make sure the young men heard and thought about my next comment. "What will you say happened to the Redbirds after that loss?" There was silence.

"Guys, you get to finish this story. It's up to you!" They were still looking at me, not sure what to say or think. "We practice tomorrow at 10 a.m.," I said. "Let's talk about the rest of the story then."

When we gathered at the diamond the next morning we got back to the story. I asked them what we would say happened after the loss. Charles was first to speak: "Coach, everybody was real upset after the loss, and they made a commitment not to take other teams for granted."

Then Michael spoke up, "They practiced harder and focused on the simple things, catching and throwing the ball." That sounded like the coach talking.

Another player said, "The team stopped listening to what others said about them and just took care of their job and what they could do. Each guy was the best he could be, and together the team was the best it could be."

These were thoughts I had shared with them throughout the season. I had hoped they would understand them. It sounded as if it was paying off.

That practice was probably the best of the season. Perhaps we needed a loss to adjust our thinking, or perhaps we just needed a goal to reach for or a story we would be proud to tell.

Each time we came together for a practice or a game, we talked about what we would say during that chapter of the Redbirds' story. And then we went out to make it come true. We never said we were going to win games. We only discussed doing the simple things. Thinking, focusing, catching, throwing and hitting. The Redbirds discovered that it's the simple things that lead to success.

The Redbirds won the tournament. The night of the championship the team had to come out of the losers' bracket. To win the championship they had to beat the Royals twice--win a doubleheader. When they did the little things correctly, they were unbeatable.

After all the congratulations, after all the trophies had been passed out, we finished the final chapter of the Redbirds' story. We sat in the grass in right field and talked about our success. Even then we didn't talk about winning and losing, only about being our best, setting our sights on success, and doing the little things along the way to make the story become reality.

It's like building life's resumé of things we have

done that will help us in the future.

I'm confident the Redbirds will remember their goal-setting lesson and share it with others. And one day you might hear the story first-hand on somebody's patio!

SOMETHING TARA DREAMED UP

While Tara was in college, she was putting together a resumé that she hoped would lead to a college internship to assist in her school curriculum. The resumé form was on a computer disk, so after filling out the initial information, she called for help. "Dad, what have I done?"

I asked her to explain what she meant.

"This resumé asks what I've done in my life, in college and high school. I put down all the clubs, service hours and honors, but it doesn't look like enough. Can you think what else I've done?"

Tara is like most of us. She wished she had done more, and in truth she was upset that she hadn't done more. I attempted to console her. "Tara, it's not like your life is over. You're only 18 years old. There's plenty of time to accomplish what you want to do. If you want your resumé to be full, you can take care of it."

Tara completed the resumé form for the college internship, but she also began work on her dream resumé. Together we started working on what she wanted her "dream resumé" to reflect when she graduated from college. She started working on it that day, writing it out, then volunteering and joining organizations to make it come true.

Dream a little. What do you want your resumé to

look like five years from now? Write it down. It's up to you.

In Tara's situation, it was a way to goal set, a fun, exciting way to create a ladder, staircase or path for the future.

A postscript to this story occurred when Tara graduated from college. She had a great resumé because of her outstanding grades and accomplishments. I answered the phone one day and it was an individual I knew who owned an advertising agency. He asked for Tara, but she wasn't home. After identifying myself, we exchanged greetings, he said Tara had sent him a resumé and he was anxious to talk with her because Tara's was one of the best he'd received from a college graduate.

I laughed to myself, and thought, "Oh, that's just something Tara dreamed up." That's exactly what she did.

THE NEXT STEP:
For both the Redbirds and Tara, it took little effort to imagine, or dream up, what they wanted.

A great way to set goals is to travel into the future, decide what you want to happen or occur, then take the steps necessary today to make your future dreams come true. Let vision lead you to success.

BEN

Anyone who has worked with young people has a special story about that one individual who stands out. This story concerns Ben, a little man I will never forget.

When Ben and his mother showed up that first day of baseball practice, he didn't want to be there, and I wasn't so sure I wanted him there either.

While I talked with the parents, most of the kids played with each other, throwing the ball back and forth. But not Ben. He was wrapped around his mother's leg. He would not let go. This little guy was afraid and he wanted to go home.

Eventually Ben stopped crying, let go of his mother's leg and we talked as we sat in the outfield grass that warm April morning. I wasn't sure where to go with the conversation, so I asked the obvious, "What's wrong, Ben?"

He got right to the point. "I'm no good." I understood what he was talking about. I remember showing up for a first practice, and wondering where I would fit in. I always assumed everyone else knew what was going on, and I was the only one who felt as he didn't fit in. I understood Ben's situation.

"Who told you you're no good?" I asked.

"Nobody," he sobbed, "but they're all better than me," pointing to the other players throwing the ball back and forth. Actually someone did tell Ben he wasn't any good. He told himself.

"Which one is better than you?" I asked, and Ben pointed to Troy, my son.

"Ben, I taught Troy to play baseball, and I can teach you. Now who else is better than you?" He pointed to David. "I taught David to play, and I can teach you."

Soon Ben stopped sobbing as we continued talking. He seemed to be a little more interested in the conversation. "Ben, let's make a deal. I'll teach you to play baseball, and all you have to do is listen and try as hard as you can. If you do that, you'll be a good baseball player and you'll have fun learning. I promise."

He agreed to that deal. He started to trust me. As we walked back to the infield, hand in hand, I didn't realize at the time just how much he was going to teach me.

Teaching Ben baseball was easy. He wasn't a great athlete, and he couldn't throw or catch very well; however, he was eager to improve. But the one thing he couldn't do was hit the ball. He just flat-out couldn't, and that's the fun of baseball, hitting the ball with everyone watching; connecting and running to first, and then standing on the base and accepting the applause from Mom and Dad and teammates and being accepted because of your contribution.

Getting a hit is what I wanted Ben to experience. He needed to stand on first base and feel successful. He needed to have that drive to push him to even more success.

I remember the first time Ben did finally connect with the ball in practice. He had tried and tried without success, but he remembered our deal: "Ben, if you do what I tell you, I'll teach you to play baseball." He tried everything I shared with him.

Finally he hit the ball--just a little roller back to the coach who was pitching underhand, but, wow, we celebrated that success! So did his teammates. They were all pulling for Ben. We needed that first connection to begin building his self-esteem.

Ben's first official hit came in the fourth game of the

season. He hit a slow roller to the third baseman and beat the throw to first. SUCCESS! I used to think that I would feel better than Ben when he reached first base, but that would be impossible because I remember him looking around and experiencing what at one time seemed as though it would never occur. Ben was glowing! He understood what an I CAN PLAY attitude was all about.

But that's not the final chapter of Ben's story. We have to go back to the day Ben first hit the ball in practice to understand his success. Later in that practice, after we celebrated Ben's first connection, Sam, a youngster who was very talented, was struggling at the plate. He wasn't having a great day. He was swinging poorly, taking his eye off the ball, and the more he tried, the worst it got. Eventually Sam bagan to cry. He wanted to walk away, but I wouldn't let him. I was attempting to get him to adjust both his thinking and his swing. He didn't think he could do it. As we were talking, Ben came running in from center field. That was unusual because the players, especially Ben, knew better than to leave their positions.

While Sam and I stood there, Ben ran up to him and said, "Sam, don't give up. I couldn't hit it when I first came out here, but I finally did it. Don't ever give up. You can do it." Then Ben ran back to position in center field--the same outfield where we made our agreement: "Ben, if you listen and try to do what I ask you, I'll teach you to play baseball."

I didn't know at the time that Ben would leave a lasting impression and a lasting lesson for me. I can still hear his words, "Don't ever give up." It helps to hear those words from individuals who understand them and then give them life by sharing them with others. People hear those words often. I use them when I speak, but Ben made them come alive. "Don't ever give up!" They took on additional meaning for me that day!

After coaching Ben that season, we each moved on to other teams. A few years later I was hanging on the fence watching Ben play for another team. His mom informed me that things were not going well for Ben. He was never going to be a great baseball player, but he discovered success through his effort when he played for me. Now he had lost his desire. The coach he was playing for wasn't much for teaching the youngsters who couldn't play. He was more into coaching the kids who had talent.

Ben caught a ball in the outfield that game. Awkward, and unsure of himself, the ball landed in his glove nonetheless. He was first to bat in the bottom of the inning. He took four pitches and walked. When he approached first base, I yelled from the fence nearby, "Great catch out there, Ben!"

He turned to me and shared that "I had it all along" look ... and then flashed a huge smile, just as he did that first time he hit the ball in practice.

Later I asked his mom if I could offer to help Ben with his hitting, throwing and catching. He readily agreed. I picked him up, and we went to a nearby high school baseball diamond. Ben was hitting the ball great! Good contact hitting, much better than he had been doing during the season. Perhaps it was because he felt comfortable. Perhaps he was with someone who allowed him to be successful. Perhaps he remembered the advice he gave to Sam.

After our workout we talked, and I reminded him what he had told Sam: "Don't ever give up."

Ben's family moved to the Northeast a few baseball seasons later. And as with so many of the youngsters I've

coached, I wonder if the time he spent on the baseball diamond would help him in life. It can. The simple lessons
work wherever you go, whatever you do. Just remember
to keep trying. Like Ben said to Sam, "Don't ever give up."

Ben is one of those special players who taught me a
lot. He's one of my all-stars.

THE NEXT STEP:

My goal when coaching is for the individuals
to understand how to transfer the abilities discovered through sports to life.

The same is true with the business audiences I
address. My goal is for them to transfer abilities in one
part of their life to all parts.

I have met individuals who use wonderful communication skills with their teams in the office, and yet they
say they are unable to talk to their children. My suggestion to them is to transfer the talents they use in their
careers to what needs to be done in their relationships.

I use circles to illustrate this point.

We often divide our lives into separate parts or seg-
ments. Like the circles. We have careers, family, recre-
ation or fun time, personal time for hobbies, spiritual time,
church. Our lives are diverse. We have multiple parts.

And each circle has multiple circles around and
within. For example, the family circle. We have our
spouse, and then our children. We might think and act
differently around each. And then our parents, our
brothers and sisters. And our in-laws, and our favorite
uncle and the relatives we keep distant. Some think of
moving in and out of the circles, as though they have
doors on them, as though they are separate rooms.

The simple fact is this: We act differently in differ-

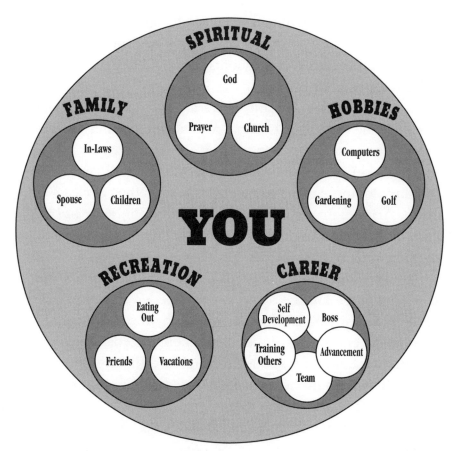

Move your talents and abilities from circle to circle. They are all a part of you.

ent parts of our lives because we feel differently about ourselves. In some parts of life we trust ourselves more than others. It is easier to display our talents in some parts. In others, we have to make a conscious effort, to adjust our thinking.

Ben acted differently in his baseball circle. Around me he tried and succeeded, but around the other coach he wasn't as successful. The surroundings made the difference. My goal for Ben is to use his talents and abilities in whatever surroundings he finds himself. Transfer his talents to all parts of his life.

This simple exercise might help you in transferring talents. Draw your own set of circles. And in each one, such as career, write your talents, your strengths. Draw all the circles in your life.

Finally draw one big circle around all of the smaller circles. The big circle is you. And all the smaller circles are just parts of you. The truth is all the talents and feelings and ideas and dreams that are in the small circles are within you and can be transferred to the other circles.

You might have a stick-to-it attitude in your hobby, such as flower arranging or woodworking. Take that attitude with you to the office.

The wonderful talents you have in running a volunteer committee are the same talents needed in running the team in the office. Communication, organization and empowerment--they are the same talents needed in raising children or helping a spouse through a difficult time.

If you know how to use your talents in one circle of life, transfer them to the others.

You are many parts, but it's all you.

TARA AND THE BIKE

Do you remember when you first tried to ride a two-wheeler? I have forgotten my first time, but I'll never forget what Tara taught me when she first tried riding her bicycle without the training wheels.

Her friends in the neighborhood were riding without training wheels, and Tara felt she was ready to step up to the big time.

Together we removed the training wheels. Her smile was huge as she first took hold of the handlebars and prepared to ride down the street to show off her new-found ability. But Tara failed to realize something -- riding a bike isn't something we just do. We have to learn to balance and pedal and negotiate the handlebars. It was going to take some work.

All moms and dads have been through this -- holding onto the bike seat while running along side and attempting to breathlessly give directions that make little sense. Meanwhile the wide-eyed youngster is discovering the difficulty of pedaling, balance, and trusting all at once.

Eventually we moved to the field next to the house so that she would fall on grass instead of the asphalt. We knew she would fall.

At first I didn't think she would ever get the hang of it. I had to hold onto her constantly so she wouldn't keel over.

Eventually she improved her balance. She started to trust herself. Her head was steady and her hands were calm on the handlebars. She was pedaling smoothly. I thought she had it, so I let go.

Tara traveled 10 feet, 15 feet, 25 feet, 30 feet. Tara was riding the bike all by herself.

Judy and I were thrilled as we watched our baby girl. "Way to go, Tara," I shouted as she rode farther out into the field.

When Tara heard me, she realized that I was no longer holding on. She was all alone in this adventure.

Tara fell. She started crying.

Judy and I went running. I felt horrible.

"Daddy, why did you let go?" Tara cried.

"Sweetheart, you were doing it. You can ride the bike!" I said.

"No, I can't," she said. "I don't know how."

But the truth is, she was riding the bike. The problem was that she didn't believe she could do it.

That young lady is just like you and me. She has talents and abilities, some she doesn't know she has because they haven't been explored or used yet. By not believing in her abilities, she didn't believe in herself.

 THE NEXT STEP: Start looking for the talents you possess which you haven't used yet -- leadership ability, management skills, ability to empower others, communication skills. Take a look inside and find your talent.

By knowing ourselves, our talents and abilities, it becomes easier to believe in ourselves.

Once you discover your talents and abilities, use them. It's as easy as riding a bike. (Although you might take a tumble at first.)

ARE YOU SOMEBODY

What a question: Are you somebody?

How would you answer that?

Working in television has produced some interesting situations for me, and often they boil down to that question.

It has happened many times in many different settings. An individual stares, scratches her head. She knows she has seen the face before, but just can't place where. Finally the question rolls out, not intended to sound the way it does: "Are you somebody?"

Today I try to work humor into the answer. "Of course I am. I am somebody."

The follow-up question is something like, "No, I mean are you somebody important?"

I think so.

I started my television career in Evansville, Indiana. Folks used to see me out shopping or in a restaurant, and say, "Hey, you're on TV."

I would answer, "Thank you." That seemed appropriate.

But I learned not to answer that way anymore. One day an elderly gentleman approached and said, "You're on television."

"Thank you," I replied.

"No reason to thank me," he answered. "I didn't say you were any good."

You learn by experience. I think he was just having fun, but I wasn't sure.

Now I know how to better respond to those situations.

I try not to draw attention to the fact I work on television. I must admit there have been benefits to being recognized, but there also have been drawbacks and some uncomfortable situations.

The bottom line, I've learned, is not to get big-headed about what I do for a living. That's just what I do, not who I am.

 THE NEXT STEP:

How will you reply if someone asks, "Are you somebody important?"

I guess the real question is "What do you think of yourself?"

People sometime tell me it depends on the situation. If that's the case, it might be time to adjust.

We have our best opportunity at success when we have a positive opinion of ourselves, an I CAN PLAY attitude, during both the good and difficult times.

In fact, it is during a difficult time when we most need the I CAN PLAY attitude. Just bring the I CAN PLAY attitude with you wherever you go and perhaps you can make the bad times good.

NEED A COACH

When the kids I coach first come together, they think I am going to teach them how to hit the ball, throw the ball and catch the ball.

As they see progress they begin to trust in me, and believe in me. They look to me for advice and guidance.

What I am attempting to do as their coach is to help them believe in themselves, and find their own talents and abilities. Instead of depending on me, I want them to understand I can't do anything for them. They are growing and progressing on their own, and they must learn to depend on themselves.

Adults do the same thing. They depend on ministers, doctors, mentors, psychiatrists, psychologists, managers, coaches, moms and dads. Adults need to be told they can be successful, that they can move forward. They need encouragement.

The truth is when we are successful it's because we have done it. There may be people who offer assistance and guidance, but the truth is we have to do it ourselves. The coach can't do it for us.

Great coaches, great managers and great parents are those who understand this simple truth. They empower others to find and use their own talents and abilities, then set high expectations, high goals for them to go after.

THE NEXT STEP:

I quit smoking with help from the patch. I was tired of cleaning smoke from the inside of my car windows, tired of looking at dirty ashtrays, and tired of feeling poorly when my children prayed for me to stop smoking. I was conditioned to stop smoking. But I needed help. The patch got rid of the dependency on smoking.

But understand this. The patch didn't do it. I did it. The patch helped.

I wore a patch for three months. I haven't smoked for seven years. I quit smoking.

Get all the help you need to be what you want to be, but realize you must do it.

Some folks think they need someone to tell them they can be successful. Some think they need permission to be successful. They think they need a coach.

If that's the case with you, I'll be your coach. Just turn to page 39 whenever you need to be told you can be successful.

You can be successful.

I just told you. It's up to you!

CHEATED

I cheated my daughter.

I didn't mean to, but I did.

Tara was born with a clubfoot. It scared Judy and me, but after a couple of surgeries, a lot of fears and tears, much care, and time, Tara walks normally, and you would have to be pretty observant to discover her handicap. For the longest time, that's the way I thought of my daughter-- as being handicapped. And I wanted to protect her.

When Tara decided to play t-ball I wasn't sure it was a good idea. I didn't think of her as an athlete. This little girl was born with a clubfoot. She would be slower than the rest of the girls. But this would be just one of the many times she would prove my preconceived notion of her incorrect.

After a year of t-ball Tara wanted to play softball. Eventually I started coaching her teams. Game after game, year after year, I attempted to put Tara in a field position where she wouldn't fail.

All the while she was developing into a talented player, but all I could see was her handicap. You might think me a horrible parent, but what I was trying to do was protect Tara.

When she was in the eighth grade I coached her school team. I was talking about positioning the girls, and the assistant coach suggested Tara in a key position. I said I wasn't sure Tara could handle that spot.

The other coaches laughed, and said, "Tara could handle any position on this team. She's a player!"

Tara, my daughter, the one born with a clubfoot?

The other coaches adjusted my thinking. I looked at Tara differently from that day forward.

Sure, I knew what she had wrong with her, probably better than anyone else, but I started looking at what she had right with her--her talents instead of her shortcomings. And Tara taught me that people can overcome their difficulties to succeed.

My daughter, the one with the clubfoot, started for her high school softball team. She pitched in summer leagues--even had a no-hitter. And she was a good hitter and ran the bases as though she never had a handicap.

She is a good athlete, and I am ashamed to say others saw it before I did. It wasn't because I didn't love her more than anyone else, but because I was afraid she might fail. I didn't understand that I would have to let her discover the discomfort of failing, just as she needed to learn the joy of success. I learned that holding back out of love is just as bad as holding back out of anger or spite.

Judy and I have pushed Tara in so many aspects of her life. In school, she was a 4.0 student in both high school and college. In fact she graduated summa cum laude. She was pushed past the things she couldn't do.

By watching Tara, I've learned not to sell people short in what they can learn and what they can do. It starts with the vision we have for them.

Today I make sure Tara knows what she can accomplish. I point out her talents and abilities. I want her to know that she can accomplish great things in her life. I want her to set her sights high and not allow any-thing to get in the way. I want her to travel with an I CAN PLAY attitude so that her talents and abilities will shine.

Tara may sometimes get tired of hearing me talk about how great she can be, but she is the one who taught me that I must continue to tell her and challenge her.

THE NEXT STEP:
   Is there someone in your home or your office who is held back because you see their weaknesses instead of their strengths?   Give everyone an opportunity to succeed. Don't limit others by what you think they can achieve.

WHO'S OUR CELEBRITY?

Humility is one of the key ingredients for great leadership. I don't think we can be leaders until we understand how to give, and humbling ourselves is a large part of giving.

Understanding that principle is only the beginning; practicing humility is a lifelong task. It can be understood through books, but it can be practiced only through experience, and, as is always the case, experience is the best teacher. My career in television and the surrounding experiences have been a great lesson in humility.

I was invited to play in a golf outing, one of the satellite golf tours. Golf pros were in town to play a tournament, but the first day was a gathering of pros and celebrities and patrons who paid to play. Being a television sportscaster made me one of the celebrities. Each team had a pro, a celebrity and three patrons.

Troy wanted to meet Jamal Mashburn, a basketball star with the University of Kentucky, who was also playing in the outing.

We arrived early and Troy met not only Mashburn, but other celebrities, including Hall of Fame baseball player Pee Wee Reese, former University of Louisville basketball coach Denny Crum, and Rick Pitino, University of Kentucky's former basketball coach--a lot of opportunities for Troy to get some autographs.

When the time arrived for the tournament to begin, we took off for our starting hole, number seven. At the tee, Troy took a look around. He saw Steve, our golf pro, and he saw the three patrons. Then he looked at me and asked, "Dad, where's our celebrity?"

Well, as soon as he asked the question he realized I was the celebrity. He was a little embarrassed that he thought of me as just Dad. But I'm glad it happened.

Every so often I need to be reminded I'm not a celebrity. Although I happen to be in a high-profile profession, I need to be reminded I'm Gary, Tara's and Troy's dad and Judy's husband.

It's easy to be humble when they're around to help me.

MATTHEW

Matthew was a young man who needed vision. He played on one of the baseball teams I coached.

I always ask the young men to tell me what they want to accomplish during the season. Some do, but most just keep it inside. Matthew opened up one day following practice: "Coach, I'd like to hit a home run!"

"Wow, Matthew, that would be exciting," I told him.

"Have you ever hit a homer before?"

"Nope," he quickly replied.

Then I asked the key question. "Do you think you can hit a home run?" He dropped his shoulders and moved his eyes to the ground. He didn't say anything, but his actions told me he didn't think he could.

"Matthew," I said, "we need to create a vision. Step into the batter's box and hit it out of the park!"

"But how coach? I don't have a bat, the balls are put away and it's just you and me on this empty diamond."

That's where the vision comes in. To obtain what we want we need a vision. I coaxed him into the batter's box. "See the pitcher on the mound, Matthew?"

"Nope," he replied.

"C'mon Matthew. Look, he's wearing a blue uniform. Number 4 on the Royals. Look, his leg is up, his arm is coming over the top. Here comes the ball, Matthew. Swing!" I gently moved his hands through the strike zone and shouted, "Crack!"

"Did you hear it, Matthew? Did you hear the ball and bat collide?"

"Nope," Matthew replied. He wasn't sure what was going on, but I wasn't giving up.

"Look, Matthew, there's the ball. It's up in the lights and it's coming down on the other side of the fence. Matthew, you hit it out of the park. You hit a home run!"

About now Matthew was ready to run up the hill and jump in the car with Mom and Dad. He thought the coach had lost his mind.

"Matthew," I said, "after you hit the ball out of the park, it's time to take the trip around the bases." I put my arm around him and we moved to first base. After touching we turned and went to second base. We stopped with

Matthew standing on the bag.

"Look over there toward the dugout," I said, pointing toward third base. "Look at your teammates, Matthew. They're shouting and yelling. They're standing on the bench with their arms in the air, and it's all for you, Matthew, because you hit the ball out of the park."

He was beginning to smile a little. He was starting to develop that I CAN PLAY attitude.

We traveled to third base, and once again we stopped with Matthew standing on the bag.

"Look toward home plate," I encouraged him. "Look past the umpire and the catcher and look up into the stands. Matthew, it's your Mom and Dad, and, yes, even your little sister, all standing and cheering for you because you accomplished something you didn't think you could do. They're standing and cheering for you, Matthew, because you hit it out of the park!"

By now Matthew was excited. This I CAN PLAY attitude was coming alive for him. He was on fire, eager to complete the trip around the bases.

"Are you ready to make the final part of this trip?"

He nodded yes and I let go. Matthew darted down the line toward home and I was running along behind, shouting encouragement. We must have been a peculiar sight out there on that empty diamond. When we arrived at home plate we laughed and then we walked over to the dugout and sat down.

"Matthew," I said, "when you can see all this, I mean really see it--the ball sailing up in the lights, and landing on the other side of the fence. When you can see your teammates cheering for you, when you can see Mom and Dad in the stands so proud of you, when you can feel the dirt churning under your feet, Matthew, when you take this dream to bed with you at night and wake up in the morning and this dream is still there, haunting you... Matthew, when this dream is with you all the time, it will push you to do what it takes to make your dream come alive."

Matthew's problem was that he didn't believe he could hit a home run. He wanted it very badly, but he just didn't really think it would come about. What he needed was to create a vision. Make it come alive. And the trip around the bases did it for him.

After we made that trip, Matthew changed. He started to practice differently. He started to practice like a home run hitter would practice. He began working harder and he had a much more confident way about himself. And he improved greatly.

I wish I could tell you that Matthew hit a home run that season, but he didn't. However he did hit a home run the following season. I wish you could have been there when he ran up to me to tell me the great news. I was standing near the concession stand when Matthew saw me. He came up to me and said, "Coach, I did it!"

"What did you do, Matthew?"

His smile was huge. "I made the trip around the bases."

It was fun watching Matthew never give up, and, more importantly, it was fun watching him adjust his thinking and start believing in himself.

Matthew used vision to decide his desired outcome on the baseball diamond.

It will work outside the baseball diamond as well.

THE NEXT STEP:

When creating a vision, make it real. Hitters in baseball, running backs in football, tennis players, they act out what they want to come true.

We can do the same in our professions. When preparing for a presentation, I imagine the individuals in the audience, how they laugh at just the right times. Perhaps my perceived expectations encourage the audience to respond.

Try it. Expect success! Not just for yourself but for everyone around you. It works!

CAN I BE IN THE MIDDLE?

I coached my children in many sports when they were young. It gave us a great opportunity to build a strong relationship. Sports was the common interest. But sometimes I cheated my own children by not wanting to favor them over the other youth. Tara taught me that I was being unfair with a simple question.

Following a softball practice we were walking to the parking lot and she said, "Dad, can I be in the middle?"

I didn't understand the question. "The middle of what?"

"I don't have to be first, but I don't want to always be last. I'd just like to be in the middle sometimes."

I was cheating her. During drills I was going overboard to be certain I didn't show her favoritism. She was always last, and, in truth, I was doing more teaching with the other girls.

From that day forward I started to treat all of the kids the same—the best, the least, my daughter, the kids I didn't know well. And I allowed all of them, including my daughter, to be a complete part of the team.

BABY HENRY

Troy had stuffed animals when he was young. All kinds, all sizes. There were probably a hundred of the critters gathered together, stacked on top of one another, in a net in the corner of his room.

Before continuing I need to share with you that all of Troy's stuffed animals talked, and they all had different personalities. Some were friendly, some rude, some were outgoing and some very shy. Each little pet had a unique voice, although as they (and Troy) grew, many started sounding the same.

Troy shared his friends and his world with all of us in the family. Although his older sister, Tara, grew weary of these talking critters, his mother and I loved this part of Troy's youth. It was easy to determine what type of day Troy was having depending on the stuffed animal he had under his arm.

The family favorite was Baby Henry. I think even Tara brightened up when this little dog was traveling with Troy.

When Troy was five he had a great opportunity. He was invited by then-University of Kentucky basketball coach Eddie Sutton to sit on the bench at a UK basketball game. Sutton offered the invitation following a conversation he and I had about our children.

The Cats were playing Georgia in Louisville's

Freedom Hall. I hurried home from work and helped groom Troy for his big event. I was sitting on the edge of the bath tub, blow drying his hair. As usual, Baby Henry was under his arm and we were discussing the players Troy would meet that night.

All of a sudden Troy held up his stuffed animal and, in that squeaky little voice, Baby Henry said, "Can I go to the game?"

I looked at Troy, and then addressed the toy, "No, Baby Henry, you can't go to this game. This is really important, and you and Troy might start jumping around on the bench and that could bother the players," I explained. "I'm sorry, Baby Henry, but you can't go to the game."

"Pleeeeze," came the request. "I'll be good and I won't jump around. I'll just keep Troy company because he might be lonely on the bench. And I'd like to meet Rex Chapman and Rob Lock." Baby Henry was putting up a good argument.

"No, Baby Henry," I said, "this is just too important. You won't be able to go."

"Please, I promise I'll be good. I'll just sit on Troy's lap. I'll be real still." There was pleading in Baby Henry's voice. And I could see that Troy was eager to see how Baby Henry's begging would play out.

"No way, Baby Henry, you can't go." I laid down the law. I was emphatic. Then I thought, "Hey, calm down, Dad, you're talking to a stuffed animal."

I'm not sure if Baby Henry had a little stuffed animal heart, but if he did, it was breaking right then. Troy wanted to take his buddy with him. We were nearly finished getting ready when Troy and his pal made their final attempt.

My son perked up and leaned forward. Baby Henry also seemed to gain a sense of confidence. Troy held the stuffed animal up to my face, eye-to-eye, and that little squeaky Baby Henry voice said, "How about if I act like a stuffed animal?"

I could hardly keep a straight face ... and although Baby Henry made a great argument, I said, "No!"

Troy's persistence and his unique attempt almost paid off for him. He didn't want to give up and he was thinking of different, unique ways to adjust the situation. I was glad to see those qualities in my five-year-old son.

When I share this story, people often ask what happened to Baby Henry that night.

Of course Baby Henry rode with us to the game. On the way, he told Troy that he was tired and thought it would be best if he would take a nap in the car while Troy and I went to the game.

Following the game, and Troy's visit to the locker room to meet the Kentucky players, I had the pleasure of listening to Troy talk to his friend on the way home. Just as we entered the car Baby Henry woke up. The first thing he said was "How was the game, Troy?"

For the next 25 minutes Troy told Baby Henry about his adventure and how much fun he had on the bench.

I'll never forget the ride home that night. Baby Henry asking the right questions and Troy sharing his world and his excitement.

Baby Henry doesn't talk anymore, except when he travels with me to a speech to share his adventure that night.

Sometimes I wonder who made Baby Henry go away. Was it Troy who grew up, or was it me and so many other adults around Troy who showed him what is expected in the "grown-up world."

I guess in my desire for him to grow up I showed him what is expected of maturity. I wish I would have shown him that it's OK to have a vivid imagination, have fun and stretch the limits of life itself.

I think it's part of living life with an I CAN PLAY attitude.

THE NEXT STEP

Today, just this day, strive to enhance the abilities, the talents and the dreams of those around you. Create an atmosphere where it is safe and OK to use imagination.

Do it for others by first doing it for yourself.

JOHN SULLIVAN

There are people who we encounter in our lives who have a dramatic impact on us. Moms, dads, great teachers and coaches are some who come to mind. Others do not spend as much time in our lives, but in a subtle way give us a simple challenge, one we can't forget and one we strive to reach.

John Sullivan ran the campus radio station during my years at Eastern Kentucky University. He later traveled Kentucky creating homespun stories for WKYT-TV in Lexington, Ky. He was loved by many.

I was asked to share some memories when John was being honored for his service to Cumberland College and the State of Kentucky. Sadly, he died shortly after this letter was written.

February 11, 2000

Wini Moran
Cumberland College
7075 College Station Drive
Williamsburg, KY   40769

Ms. Moran,

My sincere regrets for not being able to join you today. When you shared on the telephone that John Sullivan was being recognized for his accomplishments, I immediately thought of one accomplishment he may not know he assisted in pulling off, namely, helping me achieve my dream of becoming a sportscaster.

I attended Eastern Kentucky University in the early 70s and had the opportunity to receive John's guidance when I worked at the school radio station, WEKU-FM. I played jazz music during the evening hours and attempted to pronounce the names of musicians I didn't know. To be honest, I had little interest in spinning those records.

I also had the opportunity to present the afternoon sports reports for the station. I had little idea what I was doing, so I did what I had seen others do--just take stories off the Associated Press wire machine and then read the sports for four minutes. I was a sportscaster.

One day, following a sportscast, John stopped me in the hall and told me he was disappointed in the way I was reporting the sports stories. "Anyone off the street can just rip stories off the wire and then read the sports for four minutes," he said. "Gary, I expected more from you. I think you can be an excellent sportscaster, but you have to put more into it."

I've been reporting sports on television and radio

for 29 years, and I love what I do. Most of all I love making stories come alive through the people involved in the stories. You can't do that by ripping and reading. You have to dig, you have to find more. I learned that lesson from a man who took the time and took a risk to be honest.

Sometimes I'm in a rush to put the sports segment together for the 10 o'clock news at WDRB-Fox 41 in Louisville. Sometimes I think I'll just get the job done. Each time that happens I hear the words, "Gary, I expect more from you." Those aren't John's words anymore. Now they're mine.

Thanks, John, for teaching me skills that have helped me in broadcasting, but, more importantly, in life.

In addition to sportscasting, I have the opportunity to do something else I love, speak professionally. I travel the country sharing my message of motivation, which is to create a vision in life, create a positive atmosphere, and take risks. Deeply entrenched in that message is to expect more from yourself.

Thanks, John, for being a wonderful teacher.

Regards,

Gary Montgomery
Sports Director WDRB-TV Fox 41

CAN'T SCRIPT LIFE!

I like structure, but I just don't like creating the structure. I'm probably like a lot of people. I want to have things organized and in order, but I just have a difficult time getting things in the proper sequence. I'm working on it.

However I like this story because it teaches me a lot about adapting, or adjusting, which is one of my favorite words.

When I started working at WEHT-TV in Evansville, Indiana, I was a weekday reporter and the weekend sportscaster. I'll never forget the first time I was live on the air, presenting the sports.

The sports director helped me organize my segment. Together we decided what the order of stories would be and then we created a skeleton script with the title of each story written on an otherwise blank sheet of paper.   As I completed and typed each story, I inserted it in the skeleton script and removed the blank sheet.

It was time to go on the air. My first time on live TV. I started with the major college coverage, moved into the local university coverage, then onto baseball. Everything was going great, and I felt pretty good.

The tennis story was next, but when I turned the page and looked down I saw the blank sheet with the words POSSIBLE STORY ON TENNIS typed at the top. My whole life flashed in front of me.

Then I thought of all those people watching me, thinking, "Look at this guy. He doesn't know what he's doing. He's lost and doesn't know what's next." I thought of all the years I wanted to be a sportscaster and how it didn't seem fair for the dream to die just because I didn't have a lousy story on tennis.

After what seemed like a lifetime, I moved the blank script page and there it was, the tennis story. It was always there; I had merely failed to remove the skeleton script page.

THE NEXT STEP:

You can't script life. You can plan, and, in fact, you must plan, practice, prepare, but the real key to success is how we adjust to the changes we confront everyday. Don't just stare at that blank page, turn it, move it and go on.

You can't script life.

BUILDING A POSITIVE ATMOSPHERE

I like to be around positive people. People who think "I can!" People who figure out how to complete a task instead of searching for reasons it can't be done. People who "never say a bad word about anybody." That is the person I think of when I say we should live life in a positive atmosphere.

They're just like you and like me. They see negative things, they have negative thoughts, but before they let their negative thoughts take hold, they adjust, they change, they alter the way they think. Everything they say is upbeat, positive. They're not just living, but sharing an I CAN PLAY attitude. They take life and filter out the bad. Yeah, that's it, they are filters. They look at a situation, filter out the bad, and they show us the way to see the good.

They look for the good!

It's that easy.

People who live life with an I CAN PLAY attitude look for the good, the positive, instead of the bad or the negative.

In my roles as a parent, a coach and a manager, I discovered that individuals accomplish more when they are in a positive frame of mind, when they are looking for the positive, and when they have a positive self-image.

I've also discovered it's easier for them to have a positive attitude when I bring one to the relationship.

But I have also met, and at times, personally have been in the ranks of those who actively want to be negative, who want to pout about life, and look for the negative instead of the positive. Their--and my--first thought is why something can't happen instead of why it can.

The problem really lies within them. They need to adjust internally, to filter out the bad, the "I can't," so they can better fulfill life with an I CAN PLAY attitude.

People who are positive can more easily identify their abilities and talents and share them with others. And it's positive people who more easily step up to leadership because most of us want to be around positive people.

It's the truth.

SCATTERED MEMORIES

Troy was working on his hitting while he was home from college for Christmas break. He was hitting wiffle balls off the hitting tee. There were about 30 balls scattered all over the backyard and he left them when he came inside. Judy told him to pick them up. She had to tell him a couple of times, and eventually he gathered them all together and put them in the garage.

It's now late March, Troy is back at college, and I just finished throwing the wiffle balls all over the backyard--just as they used to be when Troy would hit them off the tee. In fact, if I use my imagination, I can recall those balls being in about the same places 10 years ago when Troy and I worked on his hitting when he was eight. Looking out the window and seeing those balls in the grass brings back a lot of wonderful memories. It's like looking at pictures from the past.

I cut the grass yesterday and for a second I thought I would get a bag and put those balls away. But I didn't, and I'm glad I didn't. This morning when I was going out, I looked over at the balls and remembered summer evenings, driving home, and the anticipation of sharing time with Tara and Troy in the backyard, throwing a ball and building a relationship.

Our tree house still stands. It towers over the backyard where the balls are scattered about. I often talk of taking it down because it needs a new floor, and the kids are grown, and nobody plays in it anymore. Judy says repair it and keep it up.

She's right. The tree house holds a lot of memories. Those memories help me keep my goals alive and remind me to help others keep their's alive.

Perhaps you have similar memories when you view a swing-set that still stands in the backyard, or a seldom used bedroom still cluttered with the stuffed animals that a child's imagination once brought to life.

Looking at the past can adjust attitudes in the present to make the future great.

THE NEXT STEP:

Have you ever looked to the past to gauge today's success? Look back at your dreams and hopes from 10, 15, 20 or even 25 years ago. Are you where you hoped and dreamed you would be?

If not, adjust, and keep working to make your dreams come alive. Remember that same positive attitude and create that same positive I CAN PLAY atmosphere you had when you first dreamed you could achieve your success!

TARA AND BASKETBALL

When I coach I try to put winning and losing on the sidelines and worry most about improving young people. However there was a passage in my life that taught me the real meaning of growth, and it was also a passage that made me a much better coach, father, sportscaster ... and person.

Tara wanted to play basketball. She had played in the eighth grade, but she knew she wasn't talented enough to play for her high school team. But she really enjoyed that eighth grade season because of her great coaches Ann and Chris Colvin. They helped her enjoy the game.

We tried the YMCA and discovered she could play for a team, but it was co-ed with 14-year-old boys and girls competing on the same level. I was sure Tara wouldn't want to play in a co-ed league with 14-year-old boys. At that level there is a huge difference in the athletic abilities of girls and boys. I was sure she would say that she didn't want to continue. But Tara is a gamer. She goes after what she wants. After thinking it over, she decided she would play basketball.

I was really proud of her decision. This would be a struggle for her since she hadn't played much basketball, but she decided she would go after it.

As the start of the season approached, I received a call from the Y because the league needed coaches. In the past I had coached in Y basketball and soccer programs, but this co-ed league didn't seem like such a great idea. After some arm-twisting, I agreed to coach the team as long as the organizers would put another girl on the team so Tara would be more comfortable.

Later I would learn there were only two girls in the league, and they were both on my team!

When I saw my team at our first practice, I was horrified. My first thought was that I was glad Tara was there. I think she may have had more experience than anyone else on the team. I could see we weren't going to make it to the NCAA finals.

But I had brought my determination with me, and I attempted to spread an I CAN PLAY attitude. It was easy to see the young men hadn't played much basketball because they lacked both experience and fundamentals. They were poor dribblers, terrible passers. They couldn't catch very well, and they couldn't shoot. And this wasn't just my feelings--they knew they couldn't play.

Tara was the most reliable player. She ran the plays properly, she worked on defense. In fact, she was the only player on the team that season to score in every game!

However, we needed to find another barometer to gauge success. Wins and losses would leave us depressed.

While walking out of the gym following our first game, I said to Judy, "I don't have the nerve to look. Did we lose by 30 or 40 points?" She looked back at the scoreboard and quietly said, "It was 40."

We kept working with those young people and eventually they started to buy into the philosophy of working hard and doing the simple things right. I think they started to enjoy practice. I know I was starting to enjoy it because I could see an I CAN PLAY attitude growing in this band of wannabes.

Our losses continued to grow, but so did our abilities. Many of the other teams had more talent, but our team started to impress people on game day, even the players on the other teams who would continually try to intimidate our girls. Our players acted like a team, seemed to be proud of themselves, seemed confident. It showed and others noticed. However, we were still winless for the season--but the scores were getting closer.

The last game of the year we played the same team we opened against. They weren't the best in the league, but they had kicked our tails by 40. I knew we would give them a much better game the second time around.

Late in the game, we were ahead by 6, yeah, ahead by 6. Unbelievable you say? You should have seen how the other team was taking it!

But more importantly, I wish you could have seen the kids on my team. They were really understanding what an I CAN PLAY attitude was all about. It was paying off. They were doing something they didn't think they could do. I was really enjoying watching them grow. Everything seemed right.

YMCA league rules required that all players be on the court for an equal amount of time. It was the rule. And throughout the season I went beyond the rule. I made sure of that.

But all of a sudden, we had a chance to really pull off something that was surprising--something you don't get to do over. And that was to turn around a 40-point loss. You must be kidding. It just doesn't happen.

Yes, the coach was awfully proud of himself. I had turned these kids around. I taught them how to play. I impressed the importance of teamwork on them. I showed them the commitment of loyalty.

But I lost it all with a minute-and-a-half to go. I substituted a young man into the game for Tara.

It wasn't her turn to come out, but I wanted to be sure of the victory. I wanted to be sure I had the best dribbler on the floor. I wanted this win. I wanted people to say, "Gary, you pulled it off!"

And Tara understood. As she walked off the court, she calmly asked me, "How bad do you want to win, Dad?"

This isn't an easy story to relive.

"How bad do you want to win, Dad?"

I had taught the kids that winning and losing is not what's most important, but I didn't live what I was saying.

"How bad do you want to win, Dad?"

I always want to win, to finish first. But not at any cost. Not at the cost of forgetting my values, what I believe in.

For the longest time I couldn't talk with Tara about what I had done. Oh, she went back into the game and we won, but it wasn't what it could have been.

Eventually, years later, I asked her to forgive me for that incident. She did, but what she taught me that Saturday afternoon I've never forgotten. Because of Tara's lesson, and my passage, I'm a better coach, a better dad, a better speaker, a better husband and a better person.

No matter where you are in your life, winning isn't worth selling out. Winning isn't worth compromising yourself. Tara taught me I'd rather be on the low end of the score and maintain what I believe than win at any cost.

My daughter was a great student in high school, straight As. But she's a better teacher!

THE NEXT STEP:

Talking about a positive atmosphere and creating a positive atmosphere are two entirely different things. I've had some great ideas, but they don't become a part of me until I act them out.

Do you have wonderful philosophies about equal treatment for everyone, or allowing others their own ideas? And do you practice your philosophies even when doing so might infringe on your time, or perhaps your pride? Or it might alter the path to your goal? The simple question is do you model what you believe?

When it comes to winning, thanks to Tara's lesson, I now know where I stand.

"HAVE YOU EVER THOUGHT ABOUT THE MILITARY"

My high school senior year was coming to an end, and I had to meet with my counselor. I'll call him Mr. Smith.

As I sat across the desk from Mr. Smith, he could see my lack of concern. He had seen it before. It showed in most of what I did around him. It showed in my effort. Most of all, it showed in my grades. He asked me to lean forward and take a look at my transcript and my class standing. My grades were horrible. I hadn't tried.

Mr. Smith then looked me in the eye and said, "Have you ever thought about the military?"

Was that it? My senior counseling session? The

only time Mr. Smith talked with me, other than correcting me in the hall?

I remember walking out of that session and thinking what a miserable counselor Mr. Smith was. He should do something more than ask, "Have you ever thought about the military?"

When I was in my late teens and twenties, I used that "counseling" session as motivation. I was going to show Mr. Smith I could be a success.

Well, the truth is I did enter the military, and it was a great benefit to me. But still, I thought, shouldn't Mr. Smith have directed me, opened doors for me, helped me, guided me, invited me to plan my future? He helped others with their college planning or their career plans. There had to be more than "HAVE YOU EVER THOUGHT ABOUT THE MILITARY?"

I entered college at 22, starting at a junior college and then graduating from Eastern Kentucky University with a high B average. I was very proud the day I received my diploma. My father seldom left home, but he traveled along with my mom to see me graduate. They never had the opportunity to attend college and probably didn't realize the significance of the degree. I was extremely happy. They were there along with Judy.

And I wished Mr. Smith could have been there. If he had, I probably would have held that diploma right in his face.

I wonder what he would think of me now? For the past 26 years I have been in broadcasting. God gave me the ability to communicate. I'm good at it, and I'm successful.

As I've grown older, I don't use Mr. Smith's words as often as I used to, but I'll never forget them: "HAVE

YOU EVER THOUGHT ABOUT THE MILITARY?" Those words pushed me to prove him wrong.

Today I receive calls from individuals exploring careers in broadcasting--TV-wannabes. Some are more ambitious that others, but they are all looking for an opportunity to step into broadcasting. It's much like young athletes I coach on the baseball field.

For some I see success. Perhaps it's their abilities or their connections. Maybe their parents know "the right people." Then for others, I can see their talents, their abilities deep inside them, but it's going to take work for them to pull it out. And they are going to have to do it themselves because they don't have the contacts, the connections. It's going to take dedication and drive. Something is going to have to motivate them.

That's when I think about Mr. Smith and his "HAVE YOU EVER THOUGHT ABOUT THE MILITARY?"

Perhaps he could see my talents, my God-given abilities, and knew I hadn't been using them. Perhaps he knew that I might be successful, but I would have to do it myself. Perhaps he knew that I needed some motivation--so he challenged me.

 THE NEXT STEP:
Challenge yourself to be the best you can be. Explore your talents and abilities. Write them down, and then explore how you are using the gifts you have. More importantly, determine how you can put those talents and abilities to better service so that you can enhance them and benefit from them.

ST. MARK'S

The first time I had the opportunity to coach I was at St. Mark's Catholic School in Richmond, Ky. Judy was teaching third and fourth grade, and I was still in college at Eastern Kentucky University.

The school needed a basketball coach for the fifth and sixth graders. They had had a team for about three years, but they had never won a game in the city's recreational league that played in the downtown rec center. Most of the young men I coached were sons of college professors. They never went to the rec center. They didn't even know the rec center existed.

I worked hard at coaching. I went to the library to learn how to run plays and how to conduct a practice. I asked friends who had played college ball. I even arranged a meeting with one of the EKU assistant basketball coaches.

I ran a disciplined practice, and the kids started to learn the plays. I thought we were ready for the first game.

When we arrived at the rec center for the first time, I was shocked. We walked in and the other youngsters gathered around us and started talking trash. They told my team what they were going to do to them on and off the basketball court, and they used words my team wasn't accustomed to hearing.

My kids were scared to death. They all gathered around me, hanging onto my legs. I guess they thought there was safety in numbers. When I took a step, 10 of us moved. I tried to pump them up, encourage them to go to the locker rooms, but they wouldn't let go of that safety. Finally I had to chase the other kids away. That wasn't easy because they were defiant.

Once the game started my team was awful. They didn't run the plays; they didn't try. They were just going through the motions. But I understood what was going on. My kids were so afraid they couldn't think, couldn't do what they had practiced. They were worried about getting out of the rec center alive!

That's when I realized what coaching is all about. It isn't about running plays or knowing how to block out. It's all about helping others believe in themselves.

Today when I take the field with a new group of kids for our first baseball practice, I know they expect me to teach them to hit the ball, throw the ball and catch the ball. I'll do that eventually. But first I need to put them on the path to believing in themselves, and trusting in the talents and abilities God has given them.

My favorite memories of that first coaching year were seeing my team interacting and having fun with individuals they had feared. Once my players gained the respect of the other teams and stepped into that new environment with confidence, they could succeed.

When we believe in ourselves, we will try new things and experience new adventures, unafraid of failure and unafraid of what others think of our efforts.

The St. Mark's kids had a great year. They finished third in the league, but more importantly, they developed the skills needed to face difficult situations, to keep going, to be themselves, to do what they knew to be important despite what others told them.

When I think of those kids, worried to death, and me trying to get them to run the plays, I realize I was ignoring what was really going on. I learned then that helping people grow has to begin within. If we can make others comfortable on the inside by helping them believe in themselves, then we can move into teaching new skills. But first they have to trust themselves.

PASSION

As graduation approached, Tara asked me to help her find a job.

"Nope," I said. "I won't help you find a job."

She was surprised I said no. "C'mon, Dad, you know a lot of people. Help me find a job."

"Tara, millions of people just have jobs, and a lot of them don't like what they do. They go to work, but the entire time, they merely put in time and can't wait until they get off. They never like their jobs, but they feel chained to a paycheck and they see no way out.

Those people really do have JOBS.

"Tara, those folks found the slot they fit in, or worst, they found an open position, and they stayed in it, even though they don't like the fit. They don't like what they do, many don't like the people they work with, and they don't like their managers. They really do have jobs in the worst sense of the word. I would hate to think that I was the person who put you in a job like that."

She agreed she didn't want to become tied to a job she didn't like.

I suggested, "What if together we search for what you love, your passion in life, and then we build a path for you to live and share your passion. How about finding a way to create a career doing what you love to do?"

It made sense to her, so we started to map out her future, actually create the perfect position for Tara, based on her likes, based on what she wanted to do, and who she wanted to do it with.

It sure makes sense, doesn't it? We're all better when we do what we like to do. Getting started is easier when we are doing something we enjoy. Hopping out of bed in the morning is easier when we're looking forward to doing something we like.

So while planning a career, why not plan on doing something you enjoy? Find the position you want and put your own touch on it. Put your passion into it!

My suggestion to Tara, and to you, is to extend your boundaries, stretch your imagination, follow your dreams. What do you love doing? What is your passion?

I love working with people, young and old, and seeing them improve, discovering their own skills. It's like coaching--helping others discover their own talents.

It's my passion. And each day my passion grows, expands, so each day I am rewriting my career goals, my dreams. It is led, not by what others suggest I do, not by what jobs or careers already exist, but by what I do, the people I meet, and the experiences I encounter.

Tara started thinking differently. She began exploring her passion. It takes some work. And it's not going to happen overnight.

But start today to create a personal road map. Take the jobs that can enable you to live your passion tomorrow.

Tara is working now toward her passion, what she likes to do. She has a map. And it's easier to start each morning when you know where you are going.

THE NEXT STEP:

My passion is helping people, coaching, instructing, teaching. Helping others see the abilities and talents God gave to them, just them, and nobody else.

Do you remember when you were small, playing as Mom and Dad watched? How you used to say, "Mom, watch this!"

Tara and Troy used to do different dives in our backyard pool.

"Dad, watch this!"

"Mom, look at this one!"

They used to drive us nuts. "I'm only watching one more," we would say, but we always watched to the very end. The kids were excited to show us what they could do. They were passionate about it.

That's the way I was while writing this book. I believed the stories, and the NEXT STEPS could help others adjust their thinking so they can be their very best. My family got tired of hearing me come downstairs with a just-completed story, saying, "Listen to this one!"

That's passion. When it burns inside and it has to get out! When you're sharing your passion, you can't wait to get back to the task.

Find your passion. Live it. Adjust it. Find a way to make it your career. You will be great at doing what you love to do. Make your passion part of the atmosphere of your life!

Yogi Berra, the Hall of Fame baseball player with the New York Yankees, once said, "It ain't over till it's over." He said this to make his team realize that you must play until the very end. Never give up until the lights go out.

It's a great phrase to motivate, to make individuals think there is always an opportunity, a chance to succeed. I use it often when I coach kids on the baseball or softball diamond. I want the youngsters to understand that the play isn't over until the ball hits the ground. Never give up until the umpire leaves the field. There is still a chance, an opportunity. "It ain't over till it's over."

The same is true for life. I know people who tell me how great they could have been, and then they pile on the excuses why it didn't happen. And now, they say, they are tied to the job. No chance of greatness anymore, "but you shoulda seen what I coulda been."

I think they just didn't let their passion grow. I think of Yogi's phrase when I hear them lament, only I think of adjusting it.

This is Gary's version of Yogi's phrase: "It ain't over till you say it's over."

What's your passion? Go get it! There's still time.

FEELING GOOD

Don Bisesi and I used to play golf for cheeseburgers. This was serious business. Neither one of us liked to lose. Don had to give me strokes. He was the golf pro at the club where I was a member.

On the first tee of one of our big matches, I sliced my drive. It landed way right in a clump of trees. I didn't talk much as I picked up my clubs and walked toward that stupid ball.

My second shot ricocheted off another tree and landed in tall grass. I don't need to do play-by-play of all those poor shots, but I ended up with a double-bogey on the hole, a six. Don had a par four.

On the second hole I sliced my drive again. However, this time I finished with a five. Another four for Don.

As we walked off the second green, Don shared some information which I have never forgotten and which has greatly helped me. He said he could predict who would be buying the cheeseburgers after our match by how I hit my first tee shot.

I thought that was odd because there was certainly a lot more to the game than just one shot. There were 17 more holes.

"Gary, you let what happens on the first hole determine how you're going to play for the day, or at least for a number of holes to follow. The secret to golf is not waiting to hit a good shot before you feel good about your game. You have to bring that good feeling with you to the golf course."

That advice helped my golf game. There needs to be positive thinking involved. And it also helps in life. As with golf, sometimes it's a fight to make yourself think positively. You have to dig deep to think you can hit a shot to the hole after missing the last three shots. But that's the secret. You have to adjust, do whatever it takes to alter the thinking part of the game.

Don was right. I always, always, always perform better when I'm positive about myself and what I am doing. That's the truth.

I think I bought the cheeseburgers that day. Thinking positive isn't going to make me a golf pro, but it will help me perform to the best of my ability. Practice also comes into play ... a lot of practice.

THE NEXT STEP:

Always carry a positive attitude with you, and spread it around. Don't wait for good things to happen to you or for you. Make them happen.

Don't wait for good things to occur in your career. Make them happen.

Don't wait for good things to be said or done in your life. Say them and do them!

GREEN EGGS

I was invited to read at an elementary school recently. I had made the commitment a couple months earlier, and when the day finally rolled around, my schedule was pretty hectic. I wished I hadn't committed myself. But it was Dr. Seuss Day, and I was going to read "Green Eggs and Ham." I like the book, and I like its message.

I read to second and third graders, and, to tell the truth, while I was there, I forgot about all the tasks I had, and really enjoyed sharing with the kids. We had a good time.

As I was leaving, the teacher said I had to hurry to get to the next class. The next class! I didn't remember committing to two classes. That's additional time which I didn't have. She said the kids would be disappointed if I didn't show up.

I called the TV station to adjust what I had to do. It would add to the scrambled schedule, but I could pull it off. So I stayed to read to the first-grade class.

First-graders are always fun. They get so involved, and they ask the most amazing questions. This was a typical first grade group, and I had a lot of fun reading with them.

But I was in a hurry. I finished the book and was ready to rush out of the room.

"OK, one more question."

A petite youngster named Tenisha stood up, and in a sweet, quiet little voice said, "Can I give you a hug?"

"Yes," I smiled. "I would really like a hug, in fact, I need a hug." And then 24 other hands shot up.

I spent a lot of time, quality time, in that classroom hugging. It really made my day.

In fact, I learned that it would be nice to hug in a house or with a mouse. I learned I would like to hug in a box or with a fox. I learned I am a person who likes hugs anytime, and even when I don't have time. I am a person who needs hugs ... I am, I am.

FAKE IT

I called my Mom the other day. She is 85 years young and a delight to talk to. I asked her how she was, and she replied, "Oh, I'm really tired today. I think it's the weather."

It had been raining the entire day. A dreary overcast, stay-in-the-house day. Those kind of days make people tired and listless. It might add to a negative attitude.

I visited Panama to speak and found the country fascinating. I noticed that the people were for the most part very happy, and carefree. My host indicated that it was because of the constant sunshine. People were happy when the sun was shining, he said.

I think he had something. It's easy to be positive in Panama.

I lived in Alaska for a couple of years. Alaska is a beautiful state, but for most of the year it's cloudy and overcast.

In the winter daylight is very short. People go to work in darkness and come home in darkness because of the limited amount of sunshine.

I have been told the state of Alaska has one of the highest rates of suicide and alcoholism in the United States. It's easy to be negative in Alaska.

I recently visited Tucson, Arizona, for the NCAA basketball tournament. The University of Arizona hosted the sub-regional tournament, and I couldn't help but notice how nice the people working at the tournament were. I have traveled to many basketball tournaments, but these individuals were the nicest I had encountered.

"It's easy to be happy when it's 80 degrees and sunshine," one parking attendant noted.

She was right. The people in Tucson were very friendly. I was told that the city experiences 345 days of sunshine a year!

It was easy to be positive and friendly in Tucson. It rubbed off from the people I encountered.

When I arrived back in Louisville, it was dreary and raining, 45 degrees and overcast. What a downer!

As I was walking down the airport ramp, looking out the window at the puddles, I thought how nice it was in Arizona. That's when I decided to fake it. I was going to pretend that I was still in Arizona. Fake it. I was going to make myself feel good.

It works. It really works. If you're not in a positive situation, not around positive people, fake it. Force yourself to be a positive person in a negative situation. If you're good at faking it, it will become a way of life.

If you have a tough time faking it, pretend you are in Tucson, Arizona. The only thing you can't fake is a suntan!

I encouraged Tara to be more outgoing. Not to be something she isn't, but to allow her God-given talents to show.

I encouraged her to be a better communicator. Tara was the type of person who would walk into a room full of people, and head straight for the corner. She was extremely cautious, and she waited until it was OK to start being herself. Sometimes she had to be invited to join into the group of people.

"Step up, Tara," I used to encourage her.

"Dad, I'm not like that," she often replied.

I knew what she meant. She was uncomfortable walking up to individuals introducing herself. She was uncomfortable stepping up.

I once told her, "Tara, you have a lot of talent and you have learned a lot. You need to share who you are, and the abilities and talents you have been given."

"I'm not like that, Dad."

"Tara, you can say, 'I'm not like that for years... when you're 18, or 28, or 38, or 48. But, Beautiful, there will be a time in your life when you say, 'Boy, I wish I had been like that.'"

People who share their talents, abilities and themselves are the people who find success, not just in riches, or money, but in comfort of life. People who can share their talents are the most rewarded. People who meet and encounter others are the ones who discover the most opportunities.

"Sweetheart, someday you will want to be 'like that.' I hope it occurs pretty soon in your life."

Then I suggested something to her. "If you don't feel comfortable stepping out, using the communication talents God gave you, then fake it. Just fake it. Although it's not you, just walk up to someone and start talking, start sharing yourself. Tara, if you fake it often enough, it will eventually become part of you, and it will be easier to fake it the next time.

THE NEXT STEP:

Fake it. Be the person you want to be, even if you have to fake it for awhile.

Just for today, fake it. Just once to see how it goes.

Give of yourself. Share your talents, your abilities, your conversation. Ask about someone else's well-being. Just try it, practice it once today, then maybe twice tomorrow. Use your communication skills.

Fake it. Pretty soon it will be part of you. That's how athletes improve. Practice, practice, practice. Fake it, fake it, fake it. Success, success, success.

Wouldn't it be horrible if no one ever found out how talented you are because you kept all your talents inside? Wouldn't it be horrible if no one ever found out how nice you are because you kept it all inside? Fake it.

WHO DO YOU LOVE?

Coaches are the people who make you better. Drive you, push you to succeed. They make you accountable. Great coaches are people you admire and want to emulate. Perhaps a better name is mentor, but coming from a sports background, I naturally think of the word coach.

Judy and I were driving down Hurstbourne Lane when I asked her, "Who do you love?" I often ask that question.

"You," she replied.

"Why do you love me?" It's a routine we often share, but this time she didn't follow the script. She didn't answer.

We traveled a little farther, and I said, "Judy?"

"I'm thinking," she replied.

We pulled up to a stop sign and I looked at her. She looked back. "Well?" I asked. "Do you have an answer?"

She said, "I love you for two reasons. You always try to do the right thing, and you help others be their best."

I looked at her and said, "Oh, no, don't do that to me!"

Judy was coaching. She was setting standards for me. I love and respect Judy Montgomery more than any other human being on earth. She has earned my respect. No, she has made me respect her. I have seen her in action for more than 30 years. Now that she has my respect, and she knows I will do anything to please her, she sets the standards for me.

Here, Gary, are the instructions I wish you to follow:

1. Do the right thing.
2. Help others to be their best.

Judy was a school teacher, and she was doing the same thing for me she used to do for her students. She was coaching. First, gain the respect of the class, then set the standards. Set them high so they will have to reach.

Judy has set the standards for me, Tara and Troy for years, by example and by action. We keep reaching to meet the coach's expectations.

 ### THE NEXT STEP:

If you don't have a coach, find one. People you admire make great coaches. You admire them because of what they do, so learn from them. Your coach could be a teacher, a co-worker, a spouse or a friend. You don't have to tell the person he or she is your coach, just follow his or her example. Decide what makes that person special, then emulate it. Go ahead, do what they do. Make it part of you. Learn from them. You might want to thank them, but you don't have to.

Coaches come in different sizes and shapes. Take the things they do and imitate them. We can learn and grow with great coaching.

MS. BAUGHMAN

It always helps when we can put things in perspective, but it's not easy to do. We have to look for opportunities to see life the way others see it. Once we do, it becomes easier for us to be understood. It's a key element in leadership.

I attended a function at my daughter's high school. It was called Mock Schedule Night, I think. Parents followed their daughters' class schedules, only for shorter time periods, so they could meet with each of their student's teachers. "Classes" lasted 10 minutes.

What normally happens is the same thing that happens to the freshmen on their first day. The parents get lost, or they are late to class because they were detained, or spent time talking with friends in the halls.

It's a nice way to once again understand what life in the hallways is all about. It puts a different perspective on the conversation when the kids talk about what went on at school.

I arrived in Tara's Journalism class and took a seat in one of the desks. When the bell rang Ms. Baughman addressed the parents. "We work very hard at Assumption to treat your daughters as individuals."

My first thought was, "OK, I've heard this before."

But then Ms. Baughman did something that made me realize she really did understand me and how I felt about Tara. "To tell you the truth," she said, "this year will be different for me. Now I really understand how important each one of your daughters is to you. Two nights ago I sat in my daughter's first-grade classroom to meet her teachers, just as you are doing tonight. After the introduction, her teacher said, 'At this school, we treat your children as individuals.' I wanted to stand up and say, 'That's nice to say, but you have to know some things about my Katie. She likes to talk a lot. She's not a bad girl, just chatty.'

'And to tell you the truth, I don't know if she can make it from the morning to lunch. She might need a snack before lunch. Katie is a little different from all the other kids.'"

Ms. Baughman then smiled. "I didn't stand up and say those things, but I wanted to. Just as you want to tell me about your daughters. Just as all the parents want to do, just to help me understand them better so that I can better help them.

"Tonight I'm telling you that I am a better teacher because I now truly understand that all of your children are individuals, just as my Katie is an individual. I will get to know each one of them and treat them as individuals."

I listened to Ms. Baughman more intently that night because she demonstrated to me that she truly understood me and how I felt about my daughter. She adjusted my perspective.

My son, Troy, also taught me about perspective, and I often use this example when I talk with youth. It seems I can get their attention a little faster when they hear this story.

I picked Troy up from school one afternoon. I asked how the day had been. It wasn't a good day for him. He explained that there had been difficulty with a friend, and he openly discussed the situation while we drove home.

When we stopped at a light, I looked at him and attempted to calm him. "Troy, don't worry about that situation. I know how you feel. It's really not all that important."

My high school sophomore son gave me an answer which was wise well beyond his years. "Dad, you don't know how I feel, and it really is important to me."

Troy was right. I learned a couple things at that stoplight on Westport Road. One, I don't have to have all the answers. (I don't have them all, and I know I don't have them all, so why would I think I have to act like I have them all.)

And, number two, it's OK to listen. Just listen. That's a tough lesson to learn, especially for parents.

WHO SENT YOU?

One of my early speaking engagements was for the Texas Farm Bureau. I traveled to Corpus Christi to speak to a young farmers' and ranchers' organization.

I arrived the afternoon prior to my presentation and joined the young farmers and ranchers on a tour of a local ranch. We had to board buses for the tour, and I was one of the last people to get on the bus. I sat next to Chad, a guy in his early 30s. The conversation was strained. In fact, it was like pulling teeth. I was an outsider in this group of farmers and ranchers, not quickly accepted.

Eventually Chad started to talk. We found common interest. He had two children, so we talked about kids and dads and being dads. Of course, I have no problem talking about my children or about parenting, but after awhile I stopped talking. I found out Chad needed a listener. He had a lot to say.

The tour lasted half the day and concluded with dinner. Just before the meal Chad and I were standing outside the restaurant. He started asking me questions about being a father. At first I was being generic in my answers, but he wanted specifics. I told him not all situations are the same so you might have to alter the way you do things. I remember saying, "Generally a parent might try ...."

He stopped me. I remember him looking me right in the eye, almost pleading. "Gary, I have some difficulties in my family, and I want to know how you would handle them."

This is the same guy who didn't talk with me when I sat next to him on the bus. The same guy who thought I was some city idiot who wouldn't be able to communicate with the farmers and ranchers about how to improve their leadership and communication skills. He had found someone he trusted and was sharing his deepest problems, looking for solutions. In me, he saw hope.

Chad and I missed dinner that night. We spent the time outside the restaurant, leaning against a couple of poles and talking. He wanted my advice on building relationships with his wife and children.

The presentation the next day went well for the 200 in the audience. We discussed communication and leadership. The two go hand-in-hand. After the presentation many of the young women and men individually came to the front of the room and shared their thoughts with me on what we discussed during our time together.

Chad was waiting to talk with me, but he hung toward the back. He wanted to be last. "When you sat down on that bus yesterday, I knew you were the speaker, and it was easy to see you weren't a farmer or rancher. I thought, 'Who sent this guy?' But after getting to know you and talking with you, I know who sent you. God sent you to talk to me."

THE NEXT STEP:

Two of the best leadership qualities are the ability to ask the proper questions and the ability to listen. If you do only one, then just listen.

CHARLIE

It's easy to make judgments about others. They usually come from preconceived notions about ourselves. When we open up our thinking about ourselves, it's easy to open up our thinking about others.

When I worked at WEHT-TV in Evansville, Indiana, I had the opportunity to host the Santa Clothes Club Telethon, a community effort to raise money for clothing and gifts for needy children in our viewing area.

While the telethon was underway, the director, Stan, asked me to talk with a visitor in the lobby. I went down the hall and saw a huge man in dirty bib overalls. Both his hair and his beard needed trimming. I took one look and headed back to the studio. Stan saw me and asked what the man wanted. I told him I hadn't talked with him and didn't intend to.

Stan said the man had asked for me specifically, and once again urged me to talk with him. After some convincing, I agreed.

The man's name was Charlie, and he had been watching the telethon in a local pool room. He reached

out and handed me a 20 dollar bill. He said thanks for
having the telethon, then turned to leave.

I looked at the 20, a lot of money back then, and I
looked at Charlie. It seemed he could use the money as
much as the needy kids. "Charlie, why did you bring the
money to the studio? You could have phoned in a
pledge."

"No, sir, I know I could have phoned it in, but I
had to bring it to you," he smiled.

"Why?" I asked.

"When I was real young, a man came to my house
and took me to K-Mart. It was early, before the store
opened. When we got to the store there were a whole
bunch of people. A real nice lady helped me pick out all
sorts of clothes, made sure I had the right sizes, helped me
try them on. I remember pushing a cartful of clothes
toward the front of the store. I never had new clothes
before, just hand-me-downs and used clothes that Mom
could pick up. I couldn't wait to get home to show my
mom." Charlie was excited as he relived this story.

"As I was going up the aisle, a man stopped me and
said, "Charlie, you don't have any toys in that basket." He
was telling the story as though he had shared it many
times.

"Toys! Mr. Montgomery, I didn't have any toys. My
mom couldn't afford to buy toys. That man let me pick
out all the toys I wanted. Anything! I was so happy. I
was excited to have new clothes, that would have been
enough, but to be able to pick out toys and games was
more than I could ever wish for."

Charlie had tears in his eyes as he told his story.
And I was wiping away tears while I listened.

"Mr. Montgomery, those wonderful people who

helped me were from the Santa Clothes Club Telethon."
He didn't have to say the rest, but he did. "That's why I
had to come down here. I wanted to make sure the
money goes to the right place and it can help someone."

I put my arm around Charlie and led him into the
studio. I got him some sandwiches and a drink. And then
we put him on TV. Charlie told his story, live on the air.

The phones rang louder and longer than during any
other part of the telethon when Charlie finished his story.

He was still in bib overalls that still needed washing.
He still needed a haircut, and his beard still needed
trimming, but I didn't notice the little things anymore. I'm
thankful I was forced to get past the little things so I could
meet Charlie.

WHAT IF I LIKE IT?

I teach kids to be hitters, not lookers. Sometimes
youngsters are content to take four balls and walk to first
base -- get a base on balls. Nothing wrong with that, but
some of the girls start thinking that's the best way to go
about their time at the plate. The problem is they aren't
learning to hit, and, more importantly, they aren't
experiencing the fun, excitement and accomplishment of
getting a hit!

Many coaches tell kids to only swing at the strikes--
the balls that cross the plate. I think it's difficult for young
players to determine which is a ball or a strike. So I
would tell them to hit the pitch they like. I want them to
be aggressive at the plate -- always looking to hit the ball,
not waiting for balls.

If we are always looking to walk to first base, we're

giving control to the pitcher. I wanted my girls to be in control -- to take control -- in the pitcher-batter situation.

We were having a dry spell during one of my coaching seasons. We hadn't won a game in a while. Perhaps our luck was going to change. In this game the opposing pitcher was having a problem. She couldn't find the plate and was walking our batters.

Linda was on deck. Hungry for a victory, I walked up to her and said, "Linda, let the pitcher throw some pitches. She might walk you."

She hadn't heard me say anything like that before. "You mean don't swing?" She looked at me as though she didn't understand. "But what if I see the one I like?"

For an entire season I had taught Linda and the rest of the team to be aggressive, and now, when it's important, I'm telling her to sit back, take some pitches. I'm glad she adjusted my thinking.

"Linda, you're right," I smiled. "I forgot that you're a hitter and not a looker. Go up there and hit the one you like!"

I always hoped the kids would develop life skills from their seasons with me. My wish was that from their time at the plate they could develop a life philosophy. If we always give control to the "pitchers" of the world -- just take what they throw to us -- then when it's time to swing, to take control, we aren't prepared. So the key is to be aggressive each time at the plate. Don't just look for the perfect pitch to hit, the one right down the middle. Take your cuts at the pitches you can hit, even if they're not perfect. Be a hitter. Get aggressive. It pays big dividends when you're called on to deliver, and you've learned to go after your goals instead of waiting for the perfect situation.

THE NEXT STEP:
I've seen my daughter and son take a called third strike in a game. Sometimes they would question the umpire's call. But deep down they always knew you don't want to give away control to the pitcher or the umpire. Take your cuts. You can't get a hit unless you swing. That's the truth.

FISHING

While speaking to a group of farmers and ranchers in Texas, I was making the point about living life in a positive atmosphere. Most of the people in the audience were fishermen, so I shared my experiences of fishing with my father.

Dad took me fishing when I was little. He usually cast out three lines. While he was setting the third line with a couple of rocks, I was doing what little guys do. I was throwing rocks at one of the other lines where it went in the water.

Well, fish aren't going to show up where rocks are flying in the water. Dad looked up from his task and asked what in the world I was doing. "Just throwing some rocks," I replied.

I'll never forget what happened next. Dad walked to me with a big smile on his face. "Gary, you're never going to be a fisherman." He laughed and patted me on the head and said it again, "You're never going to be a fisherman."

My dad told that story a couple of thousand times in his life. I know I heard it at least a thousand. "Gary, you're never going to be a fisherman."

It turned out to be true. I'm not a fisherman. I've been told all my life that I wasn't going to be a fisherman, and I believed it.

I try to remember that story when I talk to my children or speak to the individuals I manage. They might believe what they are told.

I also need to remember the story for myself. I too will believe what I'm told. Most importantly, I'll believe what I tell myself.

THE NEXT STEP:

What do you tell yourself you can and can't do? What kind of atmosphere do you live in? Is there something you were told you can't do, and then started to believe it?

Make a conscious effort to adjust. For the rest of the day, get rid of negative talk. Eventually you'll get rid of negative thoughts.

Today I'm going to convince myself that I can make those putts on the golf course.

Note: I told the fishing story to a group of farmers in Arkansas and made the point that I'm not a fisherman. One fella yelled out, "Well, don't blame your dad!"

He's right. Perhaps someone else might create an atmosphere around you, but you decide what you are, how you think and what you are going to be.

FATHER GRINER

I attended a workshop at my church for lectors, people who read scripture during the service. Father Bill Griner led the workshop and asked a very simple question:

"What makes a great lector?" he asked.

Everybody had an answer. In fact Fr. Griner required an answer.

"Great eye contact," was one answer.

"A good speaking voice," was another response.

Many different answers. Most of them pretty good.

"Read slowly. Don't move around too much. Work hard to prepare in advance." The individuals had wonderful ideas about how to become a great lector.

Fr. Griner listened to each response, about 40 in all. He nodded to each person, agreeing with their idea.

He was like a fourth grade teacher, allowing everyone a turn, calmly waiting, but doubting anyone would have the answer he was looking for.

Finally after everyone responded, Fr. Griner walked over and picked up the Bible. "When you believe what is in this book," he said, "you will be a great lector."

That was a revelation. When you believe what you are saying, you will say it better. When you live what you believe, you will live life more comfortably.

And in life, relationships and careers, when you know who you are and what you believe, you will be better at what you do. Plus it will be easier to trust yourself if you know what you trust.

That's part of living life with an "I CAN PLAY" attitude!

THE NEXT STEP:

Quit working so hard on the exterior things in life, and work on the interior -- things like integrity, beliefs, and values. Once you define who you are and what you believe, goals and direction will be easier to determine. When you know who is guiding the ship, you'll always know which way to turn.

Risks are easier to take once you believe the step you are taking is the right step.

TAKING RISKS

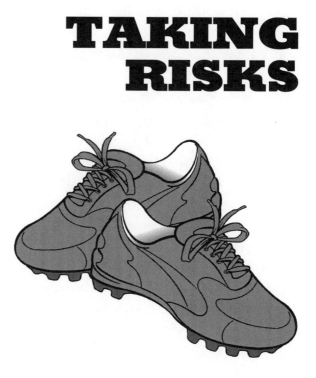

The person with an I CAN PLAY attitude looks for opportunities to risk and opportunities to fail.

That may sound peculiar, but when you risk, you have the opportunity to be successful or unsuccessful.

What stops most individuals is that they see the opportunity to be unsuccessful as greater than the opportunity to succeed. So their fear of failure stops them from trying.

Individuals with an I CAN PLAY attitude see setbacks, or momentary failures, merely as learning experiences -- chances to get closer to success.

Once the I CAN PLAY attitude grows inside a person, he or she wakes up in the morning and goes looking for the chance to fail. It puts them closer to the success they are seeking.

People who live with an I CAN PLAY attitude are on an adventure. It's called life, and the more times you risk, the more you step out, the more opportunities you have to be successful on the adventure. It's a conscious effort to advance.

Successful individuals, the ones advancing in their careers and their relationships, have taken risks, failed, and risked again.

They see life as a continual adventure -- not trying to get ready, not waiting for the right time, but constantly risking while living life with an I CAN PLAY attitude.

THE GO-TO GUY

In sports, in the office and in life, there are go-to guys -- people you know you can depend on to get the job done. I think most people would like to be the go-to person in their organization.

My son was on his high school junior varsity baseball team, and during a ride home from practice, we were talking about the team and the upcoming season when I asked him, "Who is the go-to guy on the team?"

"What do you mean, Dad?" he asked.

"The guy you can always depend on. The guy you count on to get the clutch hit or make the play."

"I guess that's Nick," he replied.

"After Nick, who would be the next guy you depend on?"

Troy realized where I was headed. "Dad, in my mind, I would be number three on the team."

I think Troy was fairly proud of his answer.

"Number three, huh." Troy nodded in agreement.

"Troy, what happens if the team needs a hit to score the tying run in the final inning, and Nick, the go-to guy, is on the bench, and whoever you have as the number two guy is on the bench, and you're the one at the plate?" Troy was thinking along with me. "If you don't think of yourself as a guy who can get the hit or make the play, no one else will ever think that way. You have to believe in yourself, right here, right now, today.

"You have to decide you are the go-to guy. You can't wait until you've had more practice, or until you perfect your swing. Too many people wait for others to get the job done because they don't trust themselves. The first step in being the go-to guy is believing in yourself and stepping up!

"Once you think of yourself as the go-to guy, it will carry over to all parts of your life. Not only on the baseball field, but in the classroom, in the hall, when your peers look to you to make the difficult decision. You'll be the go-to guy when you need the courage to trust yourself and do what you believe in. Your peers will listen to you, and go to you for advice, and you can assist them in making right choices"

That's what leaders do. When it's time to make the decision, they stand up and decide to be the go-to guy.

If you don't think it can happen, it won't. It all starts with what you think of yourself.

Being the go-to guy is just like having an I CAN PLAY attitude!

THE NEXT STEP:

Make a conscious effort to contribute what you have to offer where needed. Give for the overall effort of the team, the workplace, the group or the family. Others will look to you for your guidance and contribution.

You don't have to have all the answers. Just contribute the ones you have. You'll be admired for your efforts.

YOU CAN'T HAVE IT
BOTH WAYS

Some people don't want their children to be competitive. They don't want them to practice too much or put too much effort into a sport. Some believe all the kids should play an equal amount of time, that it doesn't matter if they win by 400 or get beaten by the same margin.

Others think winning is everything. You must win. You must practice daily. At all cost you should make winning the most important product of what you do. Beating people is important.

I fall somewhere in the middle of those ideas. As a coach, a manager and a dad, I constantly question what is most important. I'm not real sure. I think the particular instance and the particular person determine what is most important--winning or just competing.

I coached a group of sixth graders in basketball a few years ago. One young man, John, was not aggressive. When he had the ball, he stayed outside. He wouldn't go to the hoop. Plenty of talent, but also a lot of self-doubt! When I could get him to commit, he would drive past the opposition and score. Once he scored, he was pleased with himself. It showed.

However, next practice he would again be noncommittal, wouldn't go the hoop.

His father was a nice guy, and during one season he taught me a lesson. It involved not only John, but his older son as well.

I practice a lot when I coach, and gym time is difficult to come by. I called an early morning practice on a Saturday, and John's father voiced opposition. He told me

I was practicing the young men far too much, that winning was not the most important issue, and that all the young men should play an equal amount of time. I guess he figured while he was at it, he might as well get it all out!

I told him I agreed that winning is not the most important thing, but I disagreed with the rest of what he said. Practice is important for all on the team, and winning is a reward that must be given the proper priority. Everyone playing an equal amount of time is not realistic, and it doesn't teach teamwork. True teamwork allows those with particular talents to use them to best serve the team. We are not all equal when it comes to our talents. The sooner we learn real teamwork means doing what's best for the team, the sooner we mature.

This parent is a friend, and I tried to discuss all of this with him in a positive manner, but I'm not sure he listened. It bothered me that he thought I was treating any of the young men on the team unfairly.

I took to heart what he said. I wanted to be fair to all, and it's difficult for kids to deal with sitting on the bench in athletics. I always struggle, and pray, to do the right thing with the kids I coach.

Later that season the same parent and I were sitting in the bleachers watching his older son--let's call him Bill-- and my son, Troy, play a game. These kids were 16 and 17, pretty good players. Bill was a great kid, but very tentative on the basketball court, similar to his younger brother. He had the talent, the physical tools, but he just didn't get the job done.

Troy once told me that most of the players on the team wouldn't pass the ball to Bill, even when he was open. He always acted as though he didn't know what to do on the court. Troy said he felt sorry for Bill, so he would pass to him, even though he knew Bill would turn the ball over and hurt the team.

This night the boys were in the first round of the city tournament. The anticipation and excitement had picked up a notch or two. Everybody sensed it was more important now.

As we sat there, I asked Bill's dad how his son liked playing on this team. He paused before answering, but then was very honest. "He likes it a lot, but both Bill and I wish the other players would pass him the ball more often."

I almost choked on my popcorn. This was the same dad who told me I practiced too much with his younger son--the young man I wanted to be the best he could be.

In my most diplomatic manner, I told him that the kids were not going to pass the ball to Bill because they didn't think he could hang onto it.

Basketball is like life. When it's important, when the game is on the line, everybody knows who to throw the ball to and who to keep it away from. The other players didn't trust Bill to get the job done. He wasn't helping the team by being on the floor -- he was hurting the team. He got equal playing time because of the rules, but he wasn't really part of the team.

And then I told him, "You can't have it both ways. If you want your children to be a real part of the team, they have to practice, they have to give, they have to earn their way on. They have to earn the respect of the team, not by being great athletes, but by giving to the team with the talents they have."

That's the truth. If youngsters, or oldsters, want to become good at what they do, they have to practice.

Sometimes when I coach I ask the parents what is important. I get different answers, naturally. They want their children to play and enjoy themselves -- just have a good time!

Then I pose this question: When their child steps to the plate, score tied with a runner on second base and a hit scores a run, what do they want to happen?

They all say, in so many words, "I hope my child gets a hit. I hope they discover the fun of success, the fun of being part of a team, and the feeling of being appreciated."

I tell them that can happen if the youngster works at it, practices to become better. That gives them the best chance of getting a hit. Just showing up and getting equal playing time will not give them the best chance of success. And success is what we're after, as a child, an adult, a parent.

You can't have it both ways--not on the basketball court, not in life. Not for your children, not for yourself. You just can't have it both ways.

THE YADDER

The tree house in our back yard is in dire need of repair. The wood has rotted and there are holes in the floor. I intend to repair it but haven't gotten around to it yet.

A couple of the young kids who live behind us had been playing around and going up in the tree house. When I saw them up there, I told them to get down because they could fall through the floor and hurt themselves.

As they climbed down the ladder, they looked at me

as though I were the meanest man in the entire world. And I'm sure they were thinking, "Why does this old man always chase us out of the tree house?" I couldn't blame them for thinking that because the tree house is a pretty neat place.

After chasing them out another time, I got the hammer and took the ladder down. I decided the tree house was too tempting and they could hurt themselves. They watched with sad faces as I pulled the nails out and removed the ladder.

A couple of days later the little boy, D.J., was in his back yard playing with his older sister. I was getting in the car to leave and heard him tell her, "There's the man who took the yadder down."

"Hold on," I thought. I wanted to explain that he could fall and hurt himself. I wasn't trying to be mean, just careful. But I didn't think he would understand. D.J. saw me as "the man who took the yadder down."

A few days later, Troy and his friends were playing wiffle ball. They had the pitching machine running, the home run fences were up and their laughter filled the back yard. D.J. was standing at the edge of his yard, watching.

While I was trimming hedges, I could see he wanted to be part of the fun. "Hey Troy," I yelled, "See if D.J. might want to help you pick up the balls after you hit them."

Troy turned, saw D.J. and invited him to help.

It wasn't long before one of the boys got a chair so D.J. could load the balls into the top of the pitching machine. And then they held him up so he could peer into the machine to see how the balls dropped into the slots before being pitched across the plate.

I went into the garage and found one of the kids'

bats they had used when they were D.J.'s size. All of us helped him work on his swing. Then we put him next to the plate to take a cut at the pitched ball. D.J. wasn't sure at first, but eventually he stepped up and he soon connected.

D.J. had a big smile on his face as he enjoyed being part of the big boys' game. To tell you the truth, he had a pretty good swing.

Before he left I gave him the bat he was using, and a couple of balls so he could practice hitting.

I'd like to tell you that I was just being nice by encouraging D.J. to get in the game, but the truth is I was being selfish. I saw the opportunity to adjust his thinking. I wanted D.J. to think differently of me. I didn't want to be known as "the man who took the yadder down."

 THE NEXT STEP:
If you want others to think differently of you, adjust. Do something to make them see you in a different light. You can't have it both ways.

BE YOURSELF

Stepping into new adventures is frightening.

I was preparing to speak to a group of very successful business women and men. These individuals traveled in a fast-paced world, and they had heard plenty of speakers and attended plenty of seminars.

I was concerned that my simple message of building an I CAN PLAY attitude and believing in oneself might not suit this high-powered and motivated audience. Perhaps I should change myself or at least change my message.

I worried about this presentation right up to the day I was to meet with them. Early that morning as I was shaving and facing myself in the mirror, I came to the simple realization that I needed to follow my own advice -- the advice I've been passing out for years. "Gary," I said firmly, "just be yourself. The reason you were invited to speak to this group is because you are Gary Montgomery. Don't try to be someone else once you get there."

This is the same message I have been offering for years. I guess I wasn't listening.

As Tara prepared to begin high school, she was worried about the uncertainty facing her. "Dad, I don't want to go to that high school. It's all the way across town. I don't have any friends there. I don't know where my classrooms are. I don't know if I'll like the food, and, Dad, there are seniors there. Everybody else will be with their friends and know where to go. I don't want to go!"

"Tara, just be yourself," I answered. "When you run into new situations in high school, just handle those situations the way Tara has handled opportunities in the past. When you meet new friends, just be Tara, the same Tara who made so many friends in elementary school. If you struggle finding a classroom, just do what Tara would do. You'll do great in high school just by being yourself."

Four years later, Tara was preparing to leave for college.

"Dad, I'm not sure I want to go. It's a couple hours away, and I won't know anyone there. My classes are spread out all over that big campus. You have to buy vouchers for meals. I don't know where the bookstore is located, and, Dad, my roommate is from Ohio. I'm really concerned about this. It's probably better for me just to stay at home and go to school. I don't want to leave the friends I have here."

This conversation was very similar to past conversations. The circumstances were different, but the advice was the same.

"Tara," I said, "just be yourself. When situations arise where you are uncomfortable, just use the knowledge you have gained in the past. Use the talents you have learned and used in the past. Tara, just be yourself, the very best Tara you can be. It's taken you a long way so far and being the best Tara possible will take you a long way in the future."

The words I shared with Tara were ringing in my ears as I looked at Gary with shaving cream on his face. "Gary, when you face that audience today, just be yourself, the best Gary you can be, but just be yourself. Don't step into new situations trying to impress someone or being something you aren't. Just be yourself. It's gotten you this far, and it will take you further."

I know the advice works, but I needed to adjust my thinking. All I could see was the new situation which was different. But the reason I was hired to speak to this group was because of who I am and the message I share. "So just be yourself, Gary. It's what you know best. It's what you do best, and you want to do your best wherever you go!"

A baseball team I coached stepped into all-star competition, and in its first game quickly fell behind. It was obvious my players were frightened by new surroundings and new competition. They were intimidated and weren't doing the simple things we all knew they could do.

After the first half-inning, we gathered the

youngsters together in the dugout and had a chat. "Guys, just be yourselves. You were picked for this all-star game because of what you've done in the past, not because we wanted you to do something different. Just do the simple things you've always done well. Throw the ball around the plate, let them hit it, catch the ground ball, throw to first, get the runner out. Just do what you know how to do. Just be yourselves."

Because they were in a new situation, these players thought they had to be different. But they arrived where they were by being themselves.

Just be yourself. That's giving it the best effort you can. It's true for those players, it's true for Tara, and it's true for me. I have advanced in life just by being myself.

I will probably forget this simple lesson again. I'll step into a new environment, a new opportunity, a promotion or a new audience, and I'll wonder how others want me to act or perform. Eventually I'll figure it out and remember the lesson: Just be yourself, Gary. The best Gary you can be.

SUCKERS

When we stopped by the bank, it was much like all the past visits to the bank. As 4 year old Tara strolled up to the teller's window, she turned around, backed up and raised her arms. She knew that I would lift her up and sit her on the counter.

She was looking around at the cardboard advertisements standing on the counter when she turned to me with her normal request, "Daddy, can I have a sucker?"

I nodded, turned to the woman behind the counter,

and said, "Excuse me, may we have a sucker, a cherry sucker?" I knew exactly what Tara wanted.

Instead of the usual affirmative reply, I received a surprise. "I'm sorry, Mr. Montgomery," the teller frowned, "we don't give out suckers anymore."

I said, "What? This is a bank, isn't it?"

The teller smiled and said, "Yes sir, but I'm sorry. We've stopped giving out suckers."

Tara heard all of this, but I didn't want to look at her. I was sure she was disappointed. "May I have a piece of paper?" I asked the teller. She gave me a small yellow sticky note.

With Tara's help I wrote on that little piece of paper, "We want suckers," and I had Tara sign it. I wanted her to know that Dad was trying to preserve her normal way of life.

"Will you see that the president of the bank gets this note?" I asked the teller. She smiled again and assured me that it would go all the way to the top!

Tara and I left the bank thinking nothing would come of the yellow sticky note. And, of course, we made a stop on the way home. We had to buy a cherry sucker.

The next afternoon there was a knock on the front door of our home. When I opened it a man in a brown uniform, a UPS delivery man, stood on the porch holding a brown box. "Is Tara Montgomery here?" he asked.

Tara heard her name and came running down the hallway. Her pigtails were bouncing and she slid right in front of me to accept the package. We took it into the family room and, as any dad would do, I cut the strings and tore the box until it need only one more slight tug. Tara put the final pull on it. Inside were suckers -- all kinds. If you wanted a cherry sucker, it was in there. If you wanted a grape, lemon, chocolate, any flavor, any brand, it was there

And there was a note addressed to Tara. "Dear Tara," it read, "we are sorry we can no longer give out suckers at the bank. In order to pay your Daddy interest on his money, we had to reduce expenses. (Now I'm the bad guy!) But we hope you continue banking with us and continue to bring your mother and father with you to the bank. Please accept these suckers as a token of our appreciation for your past and future visits."

The president of that bank built a relationship with me. I continue to bank there and plan to always bank there, simply because he took the time to read that note, and he read it with more than just his eyes. By way of a yellow sticky note, he developed a relationship with someone he had never met. People who are successful, individuals with an I CAN PLAY attitude are like the bank president. They use all their senses in developing and building relationships.

Great salespersons understand this simple process of building relationships. Great moms, great dads, great friends, great people understand this process of building relationships that will withstand the test of time, and the trials of everyday life.

Building relationships is all about giving yourself away. People who believe in themselves have no problem giving because they expect nothing in return. They think only of helping or giving service to someone else.

FOR A DOLLAR

I was working for the Louisville Fire Department in 1970 when I decided to become a sportscaster.

I recall telling the guys I worked with that I was going to college and become a sportscaster. They had heard it so often, they didn't believe me.

I remember sitting in front of the firehouse one evening and hearing Captain Gaines say, "Montgomery, you aren't going anywhere. You'll always be at the firehouse just like the rest of us. You'll retire from here. You aren't going anywhere."

Not going anywhere? I better get going, I thought. Stop talking and do something.

My plan was charted. The first step was college. Night school seemed the way to go.

After exploring that path I found I had to adjust. As a firefighter I worked 24 hours on and had 48 hours off. When classes fell on the nights I worked, I would have to make trades with guys on other shifts. That's a lot of trades. I decided I would leave the fire department and get a job during the day.

Once I made the decision, I went to headquarters and turned in my two-weeks notice. I felt good about my decision but at the same time, a little apprehensive. Riding home I asked myself these question and others which made me a little uncomfortable. What if college wasn't for me? What if I found out I didn't have what it takes to be a sportscaster?

But then I thought, I could always go back to being a fireman if it didn't work out.

What? If I'm planning on failing and returning to the firehouse, why leave in the first place?

I adjusted my thinking real quick.

When I went back to the firehouse, I offered all of my fire equipment for sale.

The equipment is issued free of charge when you first join, but if you ever leave and then re-join the fire department you must purchase your own, so most people hang onto their equipment. I wasn't very good at saving money, so I didn't plan on having the hundreds of dollars it took to purchase the gear. Selling everything was cutting the string that attached me to the fire department. It was trusting in my abilities and believing in what I could accomplish. I was going to become a sportscaster.

So I sold my equipment, everything - fire jacket, helmet, night hawks (the pants and boots that sit at the end of the bed ready for jumping into in the middle of the night.) All the equipment was gone. Returning to the fire department was no longer an option for me. I had to look forward, not back.

I found a day job with the Louisville Gas and Electric Company as a rigger. I helped build a power station just outside town along the Ohio River.

One January morning I was riding over to the train yard to pick up steel. I was sitting on the back of a flat-bed truck along with the rest of my gang, seven guys. We were traveling about 40 miles an hour, in 10-degree temperatures, with nothing blocking the wind. I was freezing.

I thought about how many years I would be traveling on the back of a flat bed truck before completing college.

That's when I started thinking about a new course of action. Adjustment is what I needed.

"I'd quit this job for a nickel," I said.

One of the guys in the gang stuck his hand in his pocket and pulled out a nickel. "Here, let's see you quit."

Everybody in the gang was laughing, just waiting to see if big-time Gary would live up to his boast. Who ever heard of quitting a well-paying job for a nickel! I really hadn't thought it out very well. It more or less just came out of my mouth -- but prompted by the thought of years and years of night school, and hundreds of long, cold truck rides.

"Naw," I said, "I need more than a nickel. I need a dollar. I'll quit this job for a dollar."

We pulled up in the train yard and the gang gathered together, laughing and pooling their money. Paul walked over to hand me the collection of nickels, dimes and pennies.

"Here's your dollar, let's see you quit." Once again, they gave me a choice, but I wasn't sure just yet.

"I don't want all those coins," I smiled. "I need a dollar bill."

Paul didn't hesitate. He didn't think I would give up the handsome paycheck I got each week for a dollar. He pulled out his billfold and handed me the dollar. "OK big time, let's see you quit." Paul and the rest of the gang figured they would have the edge on me for quite a while with this episode. They knew I wouldn't quit.

I took the dollar. "I'll quit at lunch, when we get back in the workhouse. I'm not going to walk in from here." We were a couple of miles out from the house. To tell you the truth, I still hadn't completely decided to quit yet. It was on my mind for sure, but walking away from that check, and depending on making it through college and then finding a job as a sportscaster seemed awfully risky.

The rest of the morning I had to listen to the guys chatter, but I also listened to me. I kept asking myself what I wanted. And I kept getting the answer. "I want to be a sportscaster." Finally I made up my mind. More importantly, I finally trusted myself. I found out that when you trust yourself, you will take the steps needed to find success. Trust is the key.

When we arrived back at the house, I went to the boss. I could hear the guys in the lunchroom telling the story. They still didn't think I would do it. But then all they could see was a weekly check. I could see more. I could see my future.

I walked up to the table to say good-bye. I really did like them even though I had only known them for four months. They were delightfully honest guys who worked hard and enjoyed having fun, but I wish I could have helped them see their own futures.

I shook everybody's hands and they still thought I was kidding. Nobody's going to give up a nice paycheck for a dollar.

Paul was most upset. It was his dollar.

As I walked to the door, I had a thought similar to the one I had when I resigned from the fire department. Well, if it doesn't work out I can always come back. Bad thinking, Gary. If you're planning to fail in school and return to the workhouse why leave in the first place? I turned back and said, "Anybody want to buy my tools and tool belt?" Every rigger had to have the tools and the belt.

Nearly everybody wanted to buy it, but I sold it to Paul. He's the one who helped me see my future by giving me a dollar and pushing me to become a sportscaster.

THE NEXT STEP:

Cut the strings that hold you back.

What is it keeping you from moving on in your career? What holds you back? What fears do you face? Keep looking to the future. Look past the comfortable present and risk what the future can be.

Keep asking. Keep doing the research. But getting ready to get ready isn't the answer. There comes a time when you have to do something.

Today is the day!

DAD, YOU DON'T UNDERSTAND

There's a lot I don't understand. My children used to tell me that fairly often. It was usually the follow-up comment when I told them they couldn't have something, couldn't do something or couldn't go somewhere with a particular group of people. Judy and I used to tell them those things a lot, so both of us didn't understand a lot.

Tara and I were having one of those daughter-father talks, and she worked herself into the "Dad, you don't understand" part of the discussion. Usually this was when she just gave up. But this time we went a little further, and we did it with this question: "Tara, tell me what I don't understand."

That's all she needed. "OK, Dad, here's what you don't understand. I'm not pregnant like a lot of other girls. I don't smoke like a lot of other girls. I don't drink. I get A's on my report card. Dad, I'm a pretty good person. You don't understand just what a good daughter you have."

Pretty good, huh -- "Dad, you don't understand just how good I am!"

I leaned forward and said, "Tara, I think you may have misunderstood me.

"Sweetheart, I promise for the rest of my life I will never compare you to the best student at your school -- that girl who earned a full scholarship to Harvard -- and I will not compare you to the best athlete on your team, or the girl who has the lead in the school play, I promise.

"But neither will I compare you to individuals who don't care about their lives, their health, their grades or what they may become. We will only compare you to God's standards, right and wrong, and how you stack up to being the very best you can be at everything you do."

Tara and I never again had the "you don't understand" conversation. But Troy and I did. I guess everybody thinks dads don't understand.

It was during a period when Judy and I were talking to the back or side of his head. Kids hit those spells, and I understand them, up to a point.

Finally I had had enough. I was ironing a shirt in the basement and Troy brushed by. I spoke to him, but he didn't respond. He came back by. I spoke again, and he had an off-handed reply, and continued walking. All I saw was the back of his head.

"Troy," I said, in my best I'm-the-dad-voice.

He turned, slumped back, and said, "What."

"Your mother and I are tired of your lack of respect. You act as though you don't care when we talk with you or ask you to do something."

Now I'm getting a disgusted look, and Troy decided it was time to set me straight. "Dad, you don't understand."

I think I've been here before. "What don't I understand?" I really believe this is the key. Ask that question
and then pretend you have no idea what comes next even
though the answer will nearly always be a response just
like the one Tara gave me a few years earlier.

"Dad, I'm a straight A student. I don't smoke. I
don't run with a gang. I make my own money cutting
grass. I go to church on Sundays. Dad, I'm a good person. You don't know what's out there, and you don't
understand just how good you have it to have a son who
tries to do the right thing."

Dad, you don't understand.

I spoke slowly because this is a time when he really
needed to understand, and he was right about a lot of
what he said. "Troy, you are a great kid, and there's a
reason. Do you recall how your mother and I were always
questioning where you were going and who you were
going with?"

"Yes," he replied.

"Do you recall how we always made you do your
homework?"

"Yes."

There were a few other questions reliving the past.
I used particular instances to recall times when we had to
adjust how he was going about life.

"Troy, there's a fine line between doing the right
thing and doing the wrong thing. And if you start to move
just a little bit off the right path, then tomorrow you might
move just a little bit more. And if you keep moving, just a
little bit, off the right path, pretty soon you're way off the
mark, and it's difficult to get you back to the right path.

"Your mother and I want to stop you before you get
too far off the mark. That's why we make a big deal out

of doing the right thing in little matters, like showing respect when talking with people, so that when it comes to the really big issues, like drugs and school work and dignity, you don't have to choose. You know the right thing, and you do it naturally. It's like being a well-trained athlete. You do things naturally, without thinking about them.

"Troy, there's a reason you're a good student, and a good athlete and a good person. You have been pushed to be the best you can be, and when you got off the right path, even the slightest move off the path, your mother and I helped you adjust to get back to the path.

"That's what we're doing now, helping you adjust in the small matters, like showing simple respect to your parents, so that you continue to be that great kid. And I know you are proud of who you are and what you have accomplished. Troy, I do understand."

He lost the privilege of driving for a few days, but he was back on track. Troy, his mother and I understood each other much better.

It's a great lesson for kids to learn and parents to share, but it has to come at just the right time, when the kids begin to tell you "Dad, you don't understand."

PUSH

I often hear parents say they don't want to push their children.

I do. As a dad, I push my children to be the best they can be.

There was a time Troy and I were discussing curfew and some other issues--things dads and sons discuss. We were working on his hitting on a baseball diamond after supper one night as the sun was going down. Just Troy and me on the blanket of green grass. It's a great venue to build a relationship and to discuss life on his terms.

We had just picked up the 40 or so baseballs and were heading back to the plate for another round of swings. I asked him a question. "Troy, do think you'll ever coach kids in baseball?"

He thought a while and then said, "Yes, I probably will."

Next I asked if he would ever coach his own children. "Yes, I probably will," he answered.

"Will you be a good coach?"

"I think so."

"What kind of things will you do that will make you a good coach?"

"Well," he paused, "I'll do a lot of things you did while coaching me." That made me pretty proud. "And I'll be sure to not do a lot of the things you did wrong." Back down to earth for me.

We laughed together and walked from the outfield into the dirt on the infield.

"Will you push your children?" I asked.

"What do you mean?" Troy responded.

"Will you push them to be the best players they can be?"

"Well, sure. I'll want them to be their best."

"Will you push them in school to get the best grades they can get?"

"Yes, I will."

"Will you make them have a curfew?"

Troy looked at me, then looked away. I'm pretty sure he was grinning when he said, "Don't go there, Dad."

The truth is our children need to be pushed.

I often hear parents say they don't want to push their children. The truth is if we don't push them, they won't have the opportunity to explore what they like and don't like.

I bet most kids wouldn't get up everyday to go to school if they weren't pushed. And I doubt they would get into the routine of doing homework each night if they weren't given some direction. (Read that pushed.)

Probably fewer kids would go to college if they hadn't been encouraged (pushed) since birth to understand the importance of an education. Kids probably wouldn't develop a love of music, if they weren't nudged (pushed) to practice when they came home from piano lessons.

It's easy to pick out the kids who were pushed on the athletic field. They are the ones with discipline, proper technique and the drive to play up to their ability.

It's also easy to pick out the youngsters who were pushed in life to be their very best.

I bet everyone can pick out individuals who were pushed. They're the ones who are continually pushing themselves to be the best they can be at everything they do as adults.

And don't worry about pushing too hard. When you love someone, really love them, you know when to push, when to pull, and when to let go.

AN EMPTY WALLET

Have you ever wondered what is going to happen in the future? I guess if you haven't, you aren't human. Everyone is concerned about the future. But not everyone faces the future in the same way. Some are worried, some unsure, but some are confident of what is in front of them.

This confidence is something to explore. Why are some people sure of themselves when facing the unknown, while others shy away from it?

I was in college during the first year of our marriage, and Judy was teaching third-fourth grade at a Catholic school. Her salary was small and didn't cover the summer months. She was paid only when school was in session. I received a check from the government because the G.I. Bill rewarded veterans who attended college. Plus I worked several part-time jobs. But the money wasn't enough to pay our bills.

One summer evening, after paying the bills, Judy reconciled our account and announced we had two dollars left and a long way to go before her next check.

I remember looking at the book and figuring that we had only one dollar left, but Judy was sure there were two. You may wonder what did it matter, but, in truth, a dollar difference would double our worth! And I told Judy that I wished we could give the money away so we could say we had nothing.

We can laugh now about our finances back then, but the truth was we never did worry about our future. We knew we would be successful.

How could we be so sure? Faith and trust. Our faith and trust was firm in God and in ourselves. We knew we had the talents and abilities to find happiness and success. We weren't sure where we were headed, but we weren't worried.

I once read that faith is similar to opening a book and reading the last chapter first. You know the outcome of the story, but you don't know how the characters arrive there.

Judy and I have faced roadblocks, fears and empty wallets in our lives, but through shared trust and faith in ourselves and God, we never doubted the outcome. More importantly, we've enjoyed every moment of the journey!

We knew we could deal with the present, overcome future obstacles and succeed.

FIRED

It's easy to be upbeat and positive when all is going well, but the secret to success is to keep that positive attitude when life seems hopeless. That's a risk!

Rudyard Kipling summed it up nicely in one line of his poem "If:" "If you can deal with triumph and disaster, and treat those two impostors just the same."

In other words, just keep it on an even keel.

We learn the most about ourselves during times of difficulty and disasters. In fact, difficulty can help us discover our strengths, talents and abilities -- who we are.

I was working for a television station in my hometown of Louisville, Kentucky. I had been a sportscaster there for 12 years. There were a lot of changes along the way, both people and management. You have to expect it.

Then the station hired a new news director. After only a couple of days, he told me he didn't like sports. It wasn't long before I discovered he didn't like the way I did sports, and, eventually, he didn't like me.

My contract was up at the end of the year, and I could see the handwriting on the wall. I was going to be fired, downsized, re-engineered, retooled.

One night the news director and I got into a heated argument. When I arrived home I tried to sleep, but couldn't. I tossed and turned in bed. I got up and went downstairs. Judy came down a short time later and asked what had happened. She knew there were problems at the station, but on this particular night, she could see that I was in a panic. "What am I going to do?" I wondered. "How will I make the house payments? How will I get the kids through college? What will people think of me?"

She was listening to a guy who had forgotten who he was. She was listening to a guy who was afraid. She was listening to Gary Montgomery who had stopped believing in himself.

"Here's what we'll do," she said calmly. "Tomorrow morning we'll drive down to the station. I'll wait in the car while you go in and resign. On the way home, we'll begin planning the rest of our lives."

Those simple words transformed my thinking. I was pulled back to my I CAN PLAY attitude. I was the same guy with the same brain inside my head. I had just forgotten who I was and what I thought of myself. I was more worried about what others thought of me, than what I knew about myself.

Judy helped me adjust my thinking. She always does.

I used to think anyone could do what I do--just present the sports on the air in front of a camera to an unseen but critical audience. Nothing to it.

There really is nothing to it for me, but there's a

reason. God gave me the ability to communicate. He gave me a personality that works well on the air. He gave me the talent to see a story, then recreate that story so others can see and enjoy it. Those are talents, and, no, not everyone can do it.

Judy taught me to see and use the talents God gave to me.

That's what a great teacher does. Helps "students" adjust their thinking to see their own talents. A teacher helps learners perfect those talents, then helps them to share those talents with others.

A great teacher also helps others see the positive when everything around them appears to be falling apart.

"JUST KIDS"

Judy and I own a children's consignment store called "Just Kids." You can learn a lot about people by observing how they handle their children in public. Some parents let their kids run wild. Others seem to understand and use effective parenting methods. Some try threats to keep control.

And, by the way, who ever thought up that "I'm going to count to three" business? It seldom works, and most times the parent seems to forget what comes after two to keep from having to discipline the child.

My favorite is when little Billy is throwing a tantrum. He doesn't want to go/stay/pick up something, so he begins kicking and yelling while hanging onto a fixture. Mom is embarrassed. As she tries to restrain Billy, she explains to onlookers, "He's tired."

My first thought is he doesn't look tired. In fact, he

looks pretty energetic. My second thought is, "Mom, the truth is he might be tired, but right now he's a screaming brat. Deal with it!"

Nearly all parents suffer through these embarrassing episodes; however, the question is how do they handle them? Sure the kids are only toddlers, not totally responsible for their actions, but the sooner we help them become responsible, the better opportunity the kids have to discover success.

I teach a class of eighth graders in Sunday School. It's easy to pick out the kids whose parents have stopped making excuses for them. Excuses like, "He couldn't make it this morning because he stayed up late last night." Or "He didn't do the assignment because he had a hockey game, and we thought that might be too much." This might be the same parent who explained away the temper tantrum at five with "He's tired." New excuse ... similar results.

There comes a day when excuses just don't work. It's better for everyone when kids learn that at three, four or five, instead of waiting until they are 16, 17 or 30. When we recognize that, we can help our children become responsible adults by not making excuses for them.

And counting to three doesn't make anything go away or get better. Who thought of that anyway?

THE NEXT STEP:

The sooner we take the risk and get rid of excuses in our lives, the sooner we can work on reaching our goals.

CAPTAIN CUSHING

I really enjoyed working for the Louisville Fire Department in my younger days. I worked 24 straight hours, and then I was off for 48--work one day, off two. Plus you could sleep while you worked, as long as there weren't any fires.

And the job was adventurous--riding around on the back of a big red fire truck, running red lights and saving people. I really enjoyed being a firefighter.

Except for Fridays. On Friday we had to inspect.

I remember the first time I went on inspection. People weren't very friendly. But I could understand why. I went into schools and businesses and told people about fire hazards, and what they had to change. So many people had exits blocked by ladders and boxes, and I would tell them to move the debris. Or they had flammable liquids, like paint or paint thinner, stored next to a furnace or boiler, or the electrical wiring might not be up to code. They would need to correct these situations.

To tell you the truth, I didn't feel comfortable inspecting. It seemed people didn't like me showing up because I created problems for them.

I was in a bad mood when I returned to the fire-house after an inspection. Captain Cushing noticed, "What's wrong?"

"I just finished inspections," I said. "People really don't like seeing me. I show them all the problems they have and what they need to do to correct them. They see me, and right away think of all the difficulties I'm going to cause for them."

"Gary," Captain Cushing said, "you're thinking wrong. Let's look at this another way. What happens if you don't discover that a business has flammable liquids stored next to the boiler? Say it overheats and explodes. What then?"

"They lose their business and perhaps someone could die," I answered.

"Right!" Captain Cushing had the answer he wanted. "And let's say that a school has a fire and they have one of the exits blocked from the inside, and the children can't get out?"

"That would be pretty bad," I said.

"You need to adjust your thinking. Instead of thinking that you're there making more work for people, imagine you are preventing fires or saving lives. Think how you are helping people by being there inspecting their property. Gary, you need to adjust your thinking."

Captain Cushing was right. I had been thinking wrong, so I changed the way I thought about inspections and conducted them. Instead of showing up with a bad attitude and negative thoughts, I started to display a positive attitude the moment I walked onto an individual's property. And I explained how we could prevent a fire or tragedy by following some simple guidelines.

People started to treat me differently when I arrived with my new attitude. As I inspected, I began to enjoy meeting, helping and educating people on fire safety. It all changed when I changed my thinking, a small risk, a simple attitude adjustment.

Captain Cushing gave me some insight on working and dealing with people in difficult situations, and the same insights work in all situations, in our careers, with difficult individuals, and in relationships with people we love.

Here are some other suggestions the captain shared

with me. He didn't offer them in this order, but generally he taught me these valuable lessons for dealing with people:

1. Get to know them as individuals. Ask them questions. There's more to people than what you first see.

2. Listen to them. When they start sharing with you, really listen so you understand what they say, not what you want to hear.

3. Always focus on solutions when working with people. Don't dwell on the negative.

4. If there is a problem, ask how they would solve it. They might have a great solution.

5. Always offer positive suggestions. Take the high road.

6. Bring a positive attitude to the relationship. It's a good idea to take it with you wherever you go.

7. When working and relating with people, like them.

I laughed out loud when Captain Cushing told me one of the best ways to solve relationship problems or to cope with difficult people is to like people.

"Cap, if I liked everybody, I probably wouldn't be having problems," I said.

"Exactly," he smiled. "It's that simple."

"But how do you like everybody?"

I think he was waiting for that precise question. "Gary, what you think of others is really decided by what you think of yourself."

I guess if you have an I CAN PLAY attitude, it's easier to find one in others.

RAISE YOUR HAND

A few years ago I was in church for a weekday mass. Father John presided, and the second graders from the parish school were in attendance.

During the homily, Father John said he needed a volunteer. Every one of the second graders instantly raised a hand. Many of them had both hands up, waving them, and some of the kids were even standing. They wanted to be noticed. They wanted to be the one chosen. Father John chuckled, "I haven't told you what I want you to do."

It didn't matter to these youngsters. They were ready for a new adventure, a new opportunity. They wanted to grow. What's exciting about young people is they understand that to go after a new adventure they need to raise their hands.

As I watched the kids waving their hands, I noticed the adults in pews behind them. Not one adult had raised a hand. Not one.

It certainly made me want to be more like a kid. And I realized that as I approach new opportunities and challenges, I need to raise my hand, step up and go after the new adventure.

And if I don't know where I'm headed, no problem—I'll learn as I go.

JUGGLE

I spoke to a group of fourth, fifth and sixth graders in St. Paul, Minnesota, not long ago, and I asked if any of them could juggle. About 90 percent of them raised their hands.

They raised their hands, they volunteered, they stepped up. I asked a few of them to come forward and juggle for me.

"How many balls can you juggle?" I asked.

"Just one," was the reply from the fourth grade girl.

"And you, sir?" I looked at the young man in the sixth grade.

"Just one," he answered.

Folks, throwing one ball in the air isn't juggling. You know it, I know it and the kids really do know it. But it didn't bother them that what they were doing wasn't juggling, and they weren't concerned what others thought of them.

They saw an opportunity to raise their hand and try something new--no telling where it might lead. I hope they always raise their hands to try something new.

THE NEXT STEP:

Do something different, something new today. If you attend a meeting, sit in the front row instead of the back. If a volunteer is needed at work, raise your hand.

Step up. No telling where it might lead.

CURT

Thank heavens for change. Most of the time I don't like it, don't want to deal with it, but thank God for change. That lesson was taught to me again the other day.

Curt and I used to work at the same TV station. He worked in sales, and we would run into each other in the hallways. I liked seeing Curt because he was such a friendly person, always asking about others. He seemed to be a real caring person. Although I never thought much about it, Curt was one of those individuals whom I would like to have think good of me. I guess that makes sense. People we like, we want to like us.

I hadn't seen Curt for a number of years until I was asked to speak at a Baptist church. It was a Sunday School gathering of about 100, and he was part of the class. Following my presentation, some folks asked questions about motivation, others wondered about some of the issues in the sports world.

Then Curt raised his hand. He stood up and said that although he had known me for many years, he hadn't seen me in a while, but he could sense that I had changed. The Gary he knew before, he continued, was somewhat hollow, without much depth, and certainly not as inspirational or caring or motivating.

I wanted to sink into the carpet while he was saying this. Curt was paying me a compliment, but the person from the past he was describing didn't sound very good. I didn't want to be that person because Curt was painting an awfully negative picture. And I must be honest, I never thought of myself as a negative person or one who was much different than I am today.

That reminded me of something similar which occurred a couple of years ago.

I work out at Powerhouse Gym, the same gym that Rev. Bob frequented. The first time Bob and I met at the gym he told me we had previously met when we had played golf together about 10 or 12 years before. After that, we frequently worked out together, and I really enjoyed getting to know Bob, a retired Presbyterian music minister. He had a lot of insight and helped me many times. His wisdom reached into all parts of life.

One morning while we were on stationary bikes solving the world's problems, he thoughtfully looked at me and said, "Gary, may I tell you something?"

"Of course," I replied.

"Remember a few years back, the first time we talked here in the gym?"

"Yes," I said.

"Do you recall me mentioning that you and I had played golf together? As you and I have grown to know each other here in the gym, and we've shared all kinds of issues, such as your careers, your family, I often think of that day we first met on the golf course and how you've changed."

"Changed? How have I changed?"

Bob smiled,"Gary, today I see you as a strong Christian, a family man who loves his wife and children, a person searching for the truth, willing and longing to give to others. Back then I saw you as a foul-mouthed TV jerk who was stuck on himself."

I wanted to hide. Bob was paying me a compliment, but all I could focus on was what he thought of me when we first met. I have always considered myself to be the second person he described.

Bob has passed away. I really miss his insight and his wisdom. He was very loving and caring. He helped me a lot. Most of all he taught me to stand back and look at life, and at myself. If only I had more friends who cared enough and would risk enough to show me the path. I try to sometime each day thank God for the ability to change and become a better person.

THE NEXT STEP:
Look for the chance to change today. Change is good. That's how we grow, physically, mentally, emotionally and spiritually.

I HEARD YOU

Giving is a way of life for some people. They constantly help others, give to others. I've helped people at times, but I didn't fully understand giving until that day in the hall at Bruce Middle School.

I consulted with the Jefferson County Public Schools for a while addressing young people in a group called Project Succeed. School administrators wanted me to motivate these selected young people who were "at-risk." They were at-risk of dropping out of school, at-risk of getting into drugs, at-risk of teen pregnancies, and, most importantly, they were at-risk of not living up to the potential God had given them.

They were a tough group. Different individuals from different schools, but they were very similar. They had heard the message "You can be great!" many times from many people. But they must not have felt great about themselves.

Each time I showed up at a school to talk with these special kids, it was a struggle. I would walk into a room of young men and women with their heads on their desks or their feet propped up. They wanted to let me know that they had heard it all before, they didn't believe it before, and they didn't want to hear it from me.

I had to work to form a relationship with these kids. Really work. I talked their language, listened to their stories, and asked what they wanted from life, what goals they were trying to reach. I played games, gave away candy, gave away money, shared my past and, eventually, most of them would come around.

Usually it took about 45 minutes to build a relationship and then 15 minutes to share the message that they could be great if they wanted to be, that they could live life with an I CAN PLAY attitude, and that they could have success in their lives, if they wanted it. It was up to them.

That was the message plain and simple. And each time I finished I wondered if anybody had heard it.

Somebody did that day at Bruce Middle School.

I walked out of the cafeteria and down the hall. Just as I was about to turn the corner, a young man pushed open the cafeteria doors and raced toward me. "Mr. Montgomery," he said as he stopped next to me, "I heard you."

I remember looking deep into his eyes. I didn't know what to say. "I heard you," he said again. Then his teacher called him back to the cafeteria. I watched the doors close behind him, then turned to leave the school.

On my way to the car, I stopped, looked back at the school and shouted at the top of my voice, "OH, YEAH!"

For days I was on a high. I felt I could do no

wrong. I seemed to walk a few feet off the ground. I felt great about myself, my abilities and my talents. I felt like I could apply those talents. I felt like I could be the best I could be. And it all came about because someone heard the message. I helped someone.

THE NEXT STEP:

I remember hearing that stuff about random acts of kindness--it works. What I didn't understand is that it works for the giver as well as the receiver.

Do something for someone -- don't tell them, don't make a production of it -- just give.

Find a non-profit agency that needs help. Actually I think they all need help. Use your special talents to help make someone's life better.

Set a goal to help a certain number of people today, let's say three. Plan it, organize it, then make a journal of the things you do to help others. Yeah, it's a risk, but you will be amazed how much you'll grow and prosper.

But you probably already understand that helping feels good. You're probably like me -- you just need to be reminded. Like having someone tell you "I heard you."

TV REPAIRMAN

During our first year of marriage, Judy taught elementary school while I completed college. I was studying Broadcasting at Eastern Kentucky University.

We lived in an eight-plex off campus and we were blessed to have 'special' security at our apartment complex -- a lovely senior citizen who lived alone in one of the downstairs apartments. Ms. Mattingly was always on the watch for what was going on around the building. Whenever a car pulled up, she always seemed to have a need to sweep outside her apartment, never saying much, just observing.

One afternoon I stopped to chat. She didn't divulge much, but was friendly. After quite a few of these chance encounters, Ms. Mattingly began to open up. One afternoon she asked about school. "What are you studying?" she inquired.

"Broadcasting," I told her, but she didn't understand so I attempted to explain. "Television broadcasting. I'm going to work on television." I thought I made myself clear.

But Ms. Mattingly heard what she wanted to hear. "I have an awful time trying to get a good picture on my TV. Do you think you could take a look at it?"

She thought I was studying to be a television repairman.

I smiled as I tried to explain, "I'm not going to repair televisions, I'm going to be a television sportscaster. I'm going to report the news and sports on television."

Too late. I could see the wheels spinning in Ms. Mattingly's head, "someone to fix my TV right here in our complex." No matter how hard or how often I tried to explain, Ms. Mattingly always heard me say, " I'm a TV repairman."

"Could you just take a look to see if you could help me get a better picture?"

I agreed to step into her apartment to see if I could adjust her TV set. I'm not a technician, but I was able to help her get a better picture by a few adjustments on the horizontal and vertical settings and moving the rabbit ears antenna.

"But this isn't what I'm studying, Ms. Mattingly," were my final words as I started up the steps.

Judy and I lived in that complex for about eight months, and throughout that time I bet I looked at Ms. Mattingly's television 15 times. You see, I finally stopped telling her I wasn't a television repairman. I finally allowed her to win. Even though it wasn't what I was, I let her think I was studying television repair. I gave in. I let her be right. It didn't hurt anything, in fact it helped. Ol' snooty, nosy, peculiar Ms. Mattingly and I had a wonderful relationship. I learned a lot about her and her life and, we enjoyed each others' company because I gave in.

I learned to use that simple lesson with my children. Sometimes I win by giving in. By letting Tara or Troy be right, even if it wasn't exactly the way it truly was. Sometimes I wanted them to know that I was wrong, and that it was OK to be wrong. After I learned it was O.K. to lose a battle once in a while, I grew closer to my children. They needed to see that I could give in to them and still be the person in charge. It's a graduate course-like lesson in leadership. It's a listening skill to allow the other person's opinion to be the one which is most important.

Great leaders understand this special skill, but most of the rest of us never learn it. It's OK to allow the other person to be the one with the idea, with the plan, in order for the team to advance.

THE NEXT STEP:
Take the risk to let the other person be right, even if you have to step back. It helps the other person gain self-esteem. It empowers

I Can Play • 137

them. As for you, you get to go to the head of the class in leadership development. When you empower others, help them grow, they will stick to you like Velcro.

Mothers understand this simple life-lesson the moment they give birth. Their goal is to help their children be the best they can be, no matter the sacrifice. Mothers just give for the child to grow. Moms understand.

Some Dads get the picture eventually, but most Dads just want to be in charge.

GOOD FRIDAY

I have often prayed and not known what to pray for. Not knowing where I was going, my prayer was usually, "God show me what to do."

I've talked to others and found it to be a prayer many have prayed. I think it might be more of a prayer for faith and guidance.

I discovered the path on Good Friday a number of years ago.

I was praying in my church, Mother of Good Counsel. On Good Friday we venerate the cross. It's an opportunity to reflect on what happened to Jesus on Good Friday, the day he was hung on a cross.

The church was dimly lit, and I was praying in a pew midway back. As I prayed I attempted to visualize what I was praying about, to make my prayer come alive. So this Friday evening, I put myself at the foot of the cross.

I looked up and could see Jesus hanging on a cross. I could see the perspiration falling from His body. I could see His chest heaving with each breath. I could see blood dripping from the crown of thorns. Jesus was real to me, so real I could see the separation of His eyelashes. I could see His eyes opening and closing. I could see the sorrow He had embedded inside. Jesus was real, right there in front of me.

As I prayed I started to feel uncomfortable. Jesus was real all right, too real. I had never experienced anything like this.

As I knelt at the foot of that cross, I prayed what I have often prayed, "Jesus, what am I supposed to do?"

To be honest, although I had a different sensation surrounding me, I didn't expect anything different that night. But I've since learned that if you pray, really search for the truth, you will find it.

As I knelt and prayed at the foot of the cross, Jesus fell off the cross, and onto me. His arms were draped over my shoulders. I could feel the perspiration. I could feel His body heaving with each breath. I could feel His warmth.

Emotions overwhelmed me, and I started crying. I was extremely uncomfortable, afraid to open my eyes. I had never been here before. I felt vulnerable.

I wanted to learn more, to continue this experience, but I also wanted it to go away. I wanted to understand Jesus and know what to do in life, but I wasn't so sure I wanted to go through this discomfort.

After awhile I opened my eyes. I felt different but everything looked the same. I continued to pray, but I was confused. I didn't understand what had happened.

On the way home I told Judy about the experience. She just listened.

The following night, the night before Easter Sunday, Judy and I attended a service at another church. She was sponsoring a young lady entering the Catholic faith. When we arrived Judy went to a gathering area with the candidates, and I went into the church.

The church was dim, and I began to pray. Just as I always did, I began to visualize my prayer. I was kneeling at the foot of the cross again, and just as on the night before, Jesus fell, and again His arms were draped around me. I could feel Jesus Christ holding me, hugging me, loving me. But the feeling was different this night. It felt good accepting the embrace of Jesus. I forgot about the surroundings as I focused only on the man holding me.

The most amazing thing happened next. As I was kneeling with Jesus embracing me, I did what was natural. I put my arms around Jesus and hugged Him. It was the natural thing to do!

My prayer that night was the most rewarding ever. And my prayers were answered.

No longer do I pray, "God, what do you want me to do?" Now I know.

Jesus is always there to love us, to put His arms around us. No matter how uncomfortable we are, no matter how much we might fear what others think, no matter how often we reject, He is always there with arms outstretched.

The question is how do we respond to Jesus' love?

He merely wants us to return the love. Just reach out and hug Him.

At first I was uncomfortable sharing this story, but I've come to understand that the reason it occurred is so that it can be shared.

A friend of mine, Steve Idle, is a minister of a Christian Church. While he and I were on a golfing weekend, I told him about my experience on that Good Friday. Steve called it a "rhema," an occurrence when God's teaching comes alive and is understood.

What I understood from my experiences is that instead of focusing on what we need to be doing, we should focus only on building a relationship with Jesus Christ. It all starts there. Once we accept and share love with Jesus, the rest of the plan will be laid out for us.

Just love, that's the simple lesson I've learned. Just love.

That's the truth.

PAPER ROUTE

I've had a lot of jobs. I've washed dishes, made hamburgers, cleaned houses, painted houses, moved furniture, delivered milk, and I was a firefighter, just to name a few of my past professions.

I was also a paper boy when I was very young, and again during my college days. Just trying to pick up a few extra dollars.

I never enjoyed the paper route. I had to get up early, real early in the morning to deliver the papers. That was bad enough. But then collecting subscription money was difficult. Folks just didn't seem to want to pay.

One evening while I was collecting, a man answered the door. "Paper boy collecting," I said. He walked back into the house for only a short time and then returned to the door.

"How do I know you are the paper boy?" he asked.

I didn't have any identification saying I was an official, licensed, card-carrying paper boy. And to be honest, I was a little upset that this guy even asked me the question. Heck, let him get up at four in the morning and run around in the rain and get his own paper.

"I guess you don't," I replied with my best college smart-aleck attitude.

"Well, I'm not going to pay you until I'm sure you're the paper boy."

From where I stood, this guy was a jerk! But I guess he had a point. It's just that I didn't want to see it his way at that moment. But, how could I prove I was the paper carrier? "I'll tell you what," I said. "When you look all over this porch tomorrow morning, and you can't find your paper, you'll know it was me who didn't deliver it."

I turned to walk away, but before I got off the porch, he paid up. I kind of wish he hadn't. I liked my solution, except I didn't think it all the way through. He could have said OK and then never paid me.

Anyway, I did get paid, and he continued to get his newspaper.

I guess that was the beginning of my customer service training.

Not everyone on my route was as difficult.

I only had that job for about three months. It had to be done just too early in the morning, and the return on the investment of my time wasn't enough.

In December I decided I would quit the newspaper business as of the first of January--just finish the month and move onto another part-time job.

Sometimes Judy would help me with the papers. To hear her tell the story, she was along every morning, but that wasn't the case. She was teaching elementary school at the time, so most of her help came on Sundays for the big paper. She would chuckle as I moaned about the early hour and the lack of sleep.

One morning as we were driving and rolling the papers, Judy saw a milk truck. "Your next job is probably going to be a milkman," and she laughed at my frown. "That's the only man in town who gets up earlier than the paper boy."

Milkman, real funny. Judy's visits to my paper route were sometimes unnerving.

The paper on Christmas morning was large, and it had to be stuffed with the feature section and advertising. Judy was sweet enough to help.

Part of my route had paper boxes out on the road, and I could insert the paper from the car, but the majority of the route required that I throw papers onto porches.

I was in a hurry, since it was Christmas, but perhaps in too much of a hurry. At one stop I put the car in "park," took a quick step out of the car and without much concern with where it went, heaved the oversized, rubber band-bound newspaper toward the porch. As I let it go, I instantly wished I could pull it back. I had thrown it much too hard.

You know how it is when you're watching something happen, and you can see the results before they occur? As I stood watching, it was as though that paper was flying in slow motion. I could see it was headed for the glass storm door.

I wanted to chase that flying paper and grab it, but no chance. The deed was done, and all that was needed to complete this mini-drama was the sound of breaking glass when the paper slammed into that door.

"CRASH!" The sound shattered the Christmas morning silence, and the storm door broke into hundreds of pieces.

Judy still laughs at what I did next. As soon as I

saw the glass break, I turned and hopped into the car to get out of there as fast as I could. It was just a reflex from my youth, growing up in the west end of Louisville -- like maybe the homeowner would think Santa threw that paper into the glass door.

Judy looked at me, and in that instant she may have understood my boyhood stories just a little better.

I put the car in park, trudged up to the porch, and rang the doorbell for some time before a man and his wife answered. I didn't have to say much; the shattered glass told the story. I assured them that I would pay for all the damage, and offered to clean up the glass. They said they would take care of the clean-up, and I left after leaving my telephone number so they could call me with the cost.

I felt stupid for several reasons: First of all for throwing the paper from that distance. I should have taken my time and walked closer. Second, for letting my past creep in and thinking about leaving, and, third, and perhaps most importantly, Judy and I didn't have money to throw away buying glass for storm doors.

A couple of days later I noticed the storm door glass had been replaced. It was easy to see from where I stood on the porch, since I was no longer throwing the papers from long distances.

That afternoon I stopped by to find out how much I owed them. The husband answered the door, and I told him I was the guy who broke the glass door. "How much do I owe you?"

"You don't owe me anything," he replied. "My wife told me what you did for her a couple of months ago when she couldn't get her car started. I appreciate you helping her get it running. Let's just call it even."

I remember helping her start the car. I'm not much

of a mechanic, but I know how to choke a carburetor when it's flooded. It didn't take much effort. But it paid big dividends.

Customer Service 101.

 THE NEXT STEP:
My next step after the paper route? A job as a milkman. Judy continues to be a prophet in my life.

LEANING ON THE FENCE

One of my favorite places to be is leaning on a fence watching a ball game.   And if my daughter or son is in the game, that makes it perfect.

There's a lot to learn from sports and competing.

There's not a better opportunity anywhere to learn teamwork than by being part of a team. I know there are those who conduct workshops on teamwork in the corporate world, but experience is truly the best teacher.

Learning to do whatever is needed for the success of the team is one of the best lessons we can absorb in life, and it's applicable in all parts of life.

Kids have a great opportunity to learn several simple truths through participation in sports:

- Practice improves performance.
- Through the risk of failure, we discover success.
- We can learn through the experiences of others.
- Goal-setting is important.
- Being aggressive isn't all bad.
- Pride comes from putting forth one's best effort.

Giving of one's self to improve the team is good.

When one team member improves, the team improves.

I guess I made the ball field sound like life's class-room. It is -- for the players and the coaches and the folks watching from the fence.

I love being a part of that classroom by coaching, but when I am unable to do so, I enjoy watching from outside the classroom, leaning on the fence.

MAKE-UP

I use makeup when I'm on TV. I've always used a specific brand of pancake makeup, Tan 2.

I was shopping at the grocery the other day and I needed to get my usual makeup, but the store was out of it.

Years ago I needed Judy to do my makeup-shop-ping for me. Didn't know much about it, plus I guess it's a man-thing. I didn't want everyone to know this sports guy wore makeup. But I've grown through that. I guess it's either maturity or a rite of passage.

I finally found a shade I thought might suffice. I also picked up a few other items, then went through the checkout line. A nice personable young girl was at the counter.

"How are you?" she asked.

"I'm doing great," I replied.

She smiled, then started running the items past the scanner. "Is this makeup for you?" she smiled as she asked the question. The way she asked I'm sure she expected me to say, "No, it's for my wife."

"Yes," I replied.

In TV we call what happened next "dead air." It's a period of time when no one says anything, but everybody wants to ask questions to clarify the situation. I just smiled.

The young lady wanted to know more, but she went about her task. Finally her youthful exuberance shot through, and she said, "You really do use makeup?"

"Yep, I really do." My reply was very casual. But our conversation had attracted the attention of many around us, shoppers in line and other grocery employees.

Finally I was about to tell her that I was a sports-caster and I used it when I'm on TV, but before I could, she unloaded with what was on her mind, "Well, if this makeup is really for you, you might want to get a lighter shade."

She was trying to offer me good customer service, but I sure wished I had the makeup on to cover my red face!

 THE NEXT STEP:
It's nice to have a little cover up sometime, but it's always, always better to be yourself -- in case the cover wears off.

STEPS

My friend Rob and I were walking up the 9th fairway at our golf course. He was playing better than usual; in fact, very well, and he wondered how long it would last. "I'll fall back to my usual game before long," he laughed.

Rob was thinking wrong. Instead of looking back and waiting for the negative past to re-emerge, he should have been enjoying the present and looking to improve in the future.

The truth about Rob's game is that he had worked on it. He had paid the price by practicing and finding different techniques to lower his golf score. That was his goal, and he was reaching it. However, once he accomplished the goal, he was allowing the negative to creep in, the doubt to surface. He wondered if he deserved the reward.

We all do it. We work to rise above our own expectations, and then once we do, we doubt if we can maintain our new level of success.

Instead of accepting success, we doubt ourselves.

I've got a theory about these personal expectations. It coincides with my thoughts on the journey of life.

Imagine yourself walking down a path and coming to a point where it splits. You have to make a decision. If you continue straight ahead, there are stairs -- very high stairs connected by short stretches of level ground. You might fail just trying to make it up the first flight of them.

Now look to the right. The other path remains straight and level. No stairs, no risk of failure. You can stay on that path and not expend the time or the energy or the resources it will take to climb the steps. But neither will you gain the experience of climbing, of developing new talents, of seeking new knowledge, of learning new skills which can benefit you farther along your journey.

You aren't sure where either path will lead. The tall stairs appear to be a real challenge, while the level path looks like the easier way. Which do you choose?

I've heard some folks describe our life journey as climbing a mountain. But I prefer the image of steps because life isn't constantly going uphill. Sometimes the path is level. Only at certain times do we encounter steps or challenges. And when we do, we have a choice. Either start climbing, trying to get up the steps, or take the easier way by crossing back to the level path where there's no struggle, no climbing, no opportunity to see what's at the top of the steps.

There is a reward for climbing. By choosing the path with steps, we develop new talents we can use later, farther along the journey when we encounter higher steps. And the knowledge we gain, the climbing skills, can't be taken away. They are always in our tool box, ready to be used. We have earned them. (Just as Rob had developed new knowledge and new skills by choosing to climb the steps and improve his golf abilities.)

All along our journey we encounter different levels and different types of steps. Some are more steep than others, more difficult to climb, and some steps are short, presenting less of a challenge. We can't predict the steps we will encounter, or their frequency. We can only prepare ourselves to be skilled climbers.

I like to think of the steps along our paths as risks. We can choose to take risks -- climb the steps -- or we can move over to the straight, easy path.

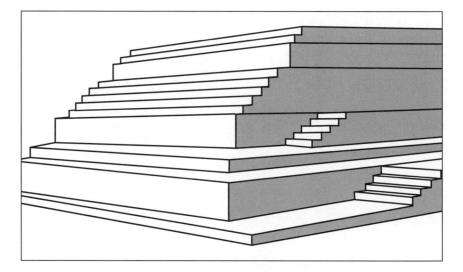

But when we choose to take risks, in fact when we go looking for new challenges, new steps in our lives, we are making a conscious effort to expand our horizons. We are choosing to grow, to add a new quality into our lives, to add a new tool in our tool box of skills, to add a new word. The word is trust.

As we become better climbers we will no longer look at the steps in our lives as risks. They become challenges, or exercise, or practice -- words a golfer or athlete might use to improve a skill. Instead of the word risk, we begin using the word trust.

And instead of fearing we might fall back to old straight-path ways, we begin to welcome the steps, the opportunities to grow and better ourselves.

We become grateful for the challenges which allow us to build our trust during the journey -- the climb -- into the future.

Gary Montgomery coaches individuals who want to develop an "I CAN PLAY" attitude for life, and teams with organizations and companies who want their associates to be the best they can be!

GARY'S KEYNOTE SPEECHES AND HALF-DAY SEMINARS

HOW TO BUILD AN "I CAN PLAY" ATTITUDE

When you create VISION, develop and live in a POSITIVE ATMOSPHERE and become a RISK taker, you will no longer be looking for success, you will be living it!

A PENNY'S WORTH OF ADJUSTMENT

Some call it change, Gary prefers adjustment. Discovering how simple adjustments can guide us to take the steps needed for career and personal success... plus, Gary lets you keep the penny!

CREATING "TEAMERSHIP"

Gary invented a word to help develop great teams. The real value comes when team members grow as leaders and maintain focus on the goal, that's "TEAMERSHIP." It's the same as leadership, but with the team in front.

"I'LL NEVER SAY 'I WISH I HAD'

Success centers itself around those who look for opportunities. How to get away from 'getting ready to get ready' and always be prepared for greatness.

To contact Gary Montgomery:

Call: 1-502-339-0040

Or write to: Prime Time Productions
              10423 Scarlet Oak Ct.
              Louisville, KY 40241

Or email: coachgary@icanplay.com

Website: www.icanplay.com

ORDER FORM

Gary's Books:

Quantity   Subtotal

"I CAN PLAY" . . . .$13.95 _____ _____

"IRRESISTIBLE LEADERSHIP" . . . .$15.00 _____ _____

Gary's Audio Tapes

How to build an "I CAN PLAY" Attitude . . . .$10.00 _____ _____

Preparing for greatness – Leadership Techniques .$10.00 _____ _____

"I CAN PLAY" key chain . . . .$ 2.50 _____ _____

$2.50 shipping/handling on books and/or tapes _____

TOTAL _____

Mail to:

Name _____

Company _____

Address _____

City _____ State _____ Zip _____

Phone _____

Please check one:

❏ MasterCard   ❏ Visa

Card Number _____ Exp. Date _____